# HOW TO CONTROL

# YOUR

# TONGUE

## 4 Steps to Master

## the Art of Mindful Speaking

## Economical Version

## ANDREAS BERKEY

**Edited by Pagetrim Book Services**

**Quote of Martin Luther King Jr**, at the beginning of chapter 12, (Excerpt from Christmas Eve Sermon, 1967), Reprinted by arrangement with The Heirs to the Estate of Martin Luther King Jr., c/o Writers House as agent for the proprietor New York, NY. Copyright © 1967 by Dr. Martin Luther King, Jr. Renewed © 1995 by Coretta Scott King.

ISBN-Paperback Economical Version: 979-8-9898859-7-8

**Disclaimer Notice:**

Please note the information contained within this book is for educational and entertainment purposes only. Every attempt has been made to provide accurate, up-to-date, reliable, and complete information. No warranties of any kind are expressed or implied. Readers acknowledge that the author is not rendering legal, financial, medical, or professional advice. The content of this book has been derived from various sources. Please consult a licensed professional when personal, direct advice or therapy is needed.

By reading this book, the reader agrees that under no circumstances is the author responsible for any direct or indirect losses incurred as a result of the use of the information contained within this document, including, but not limited to, errors, omissions, or inaccuracies.

Comments, suggestions, and recommendations are welcome and may be sent by email to admin@AndreasBerkey.com

# CONTENTS

# TO FREEDOM

# INTRODUCTION

"It happens to the best of us."

That's what a colleague told me as I sat alone in my office, my emotions still raw after a heated verbal encounter with some staff members. I wanted so desperately to believe her, but all I could think about was how I wished the ground would open up and swallow me whole.

I am a physician in a busy urgent care and community clinic that takes all comers. We turn no one away. Under the best of circumstances, we balance the need to provide quality care with the need to be available to thousands of patients per provider. On top of this, during the Covid-19 pandemic, healthcare workers everywhere were asked to do more with less. Many staff quit. Protective gear was in short supply. Longer workdays were required. We often ran out of personnel and critical supplies. Everyone in our clinic and in need of urgent care felt the strain. While the mantra of "business as usual" was still chanted, some employees could only muster their bare minimum, adversely affecting the quality of the care we gave to patients. This frustrated me to no end.

In retrospect, I can see I expressed frustration impulsively, swear words included. I plead guilty! Though accepted and even encouraged in some job environments, such expressions are forbidden in most healthcare settings. I spoke without counting the cost. Regardless of the cause, it was an eye-opening moment for me. I wondered if and how I could prevent it from happening again. My boss made it clear that if it did happen again, I would be let go. I would be fired. And I couldn't afford that!

During that first year of the pandemic, anyone in service industries who could afford to quit did so. It wasn't just in clinics and hospitals. Pharmacists and pharmacy techs made international news for nearly going nuts. They had less staff, but they were given the added responsibility of vaccinating a mass influx of people. Like other service workers, those remaining in healthcare were called upon to work harder and longer. Some took up the challenge. Initially, I was angry at those who did not.

Finally, two years later, I can honestly say I no longer bear anger towards those who took the opposite approach. Some employees felt the best way to survive was to do the minimum required and keep a low profile. That was my assessment; maybe I do not know what they truly felt. I cannot control that anyway. Our response to the stress differed. It's as simple as that.

It took me a while to figure out that not everyone shared my work ethic. Some worked harder than me. Others, much less. At the time, when I witnessed those doing the bare minimum, I quickly judged them as careless, irresponsible, and disrespectful. And even if my assessment was right in some cases, my response only hindered productivity.

The details of my swearing torrent in the workplace have become blurry in my memory, but the pain and confusion I caused by letting my emotions get the best of me remain all too clear.

The swear words I uttered were aimed at no one in particular. However, they did not fit the culture of our workplace. My frustrated outburst was offensive to one or more persons. That's all it took to get me into trouble, no matter how hard I was working for the team. It did not help that I superseded my colorful language with a sarcastic monologue about the quality of care we were providing. What was the purpose? To demand the work standards I upheld. Did I achieve what I wanted? No. I only managed to offend a few individuals, disrupt the work dynamics, taint my reputation, and nearly lose my job.

As I reflected on this incident, I recognized the need for a shift in my communication approach. I pondered the impact of my impulsive words and how they had harmed, rather than helped, my cause.

Every workplace has its own culture. While doing research on how to control one's tongue, I stumbled across peer-reviewed research that demonstrated that in proper context, swearing in the workplace can be a good thing. But more about that later.

As it turns out, I am not the only one to misjudge what speech is appropriate or not. Spoken words are like ink on a page, leaving a lasting impression. It wasn't until I acknowledged the consequences of my verbal tirade that I could look inwards to know where these words originated from and look outwards for mentors or counselors who could help me improve.

The more I learned, the more I reconnected with the healing power of words. I set a goal to master the delicate art of controlling my tongue, ensuring every word spoken is imbued with empathy and consideration. I am by no means perfect in this journey. I only hope that I am among the most improved and that I can share that with you.

The purpose of this book is to share what I and others have learned about mastering the art of mindful speaking, focusing on face-to-face speaking and listening.

Usage and reliance on ever-evolving media technology has affected our communication in many ways. In today's fast-paced digital landscape, the perils of hasty communication and impulsive remarks resonate more than ever. With the rise of social media and instant messaging, individuals often find themselves entangled in virtual dialogues that quickly escalate into tense, often toxic, territory.

This was certainly the case during the pandemic when people were confined to their homes and the only outlet to vent their frustrations was through their social media portals, inviting faceless trolls to join in heated digital debates and causing division and angst.

It is no secret that the allure of a witty comment or snappy comeback can be hard to resist, especially when discussions veer towards sensitive topics. In the race to be heard, the online space frequently witnesses the inadvertent trampling of opposing viewpoints. The result? Escalating conflicts, fractured relationships, and a pervasive, hostile atmosphere.

Even as platforms strive to promote dialogue, they often fuel misunderstandings and intensify polarization. The need to acknowledge the power of listening over speaking and understanding over rebutting is critical, as the virtual realm demands a conscious effort to bridge gaps rather than widen them.

Indeed, in face-to-face interactions, the challenges of maintaining mindful communication remain just as prevalent, as exemplified by the unfortunate incident I shared.

Conversations within communities, workplaces, and households reflect the need for thoughtful dialogue and empathetic understanding. With societal divisions deepening and sensitive issues pervading everyday discourse, the need for respectful engagement is crucial.

Overshadowed by the temptation of witty banter and the need to assert one's perspective, individuals frequently find themselves entangled in verbal conflicts that can strain relationships and sow seeds of hatred. The tendency to speak before fully comprehending the nuances of a situation often leads to unintended misunderstandings and hurt feelings.

New forms of communication always bring new challenges. When telephones were invented, there was a corresponding loss of visual cues. Now we have texting, video chats, group video teleconferencing, and telemedicine doctor visits. Undoubtedly, new and exciting forms of communication will come. Maybe holographic projections will replace flat screen video calls. I don't know. But what I do know is each form will have its own set of nuances that will add or take away from its predecessor. What will remain unchanged is our desire to be respected and treated kindly.

The importance of listening, acknowledging diverse viewpoints, and learning when to pause in face-to-face exchanges cannot be overstated.

*How to Control your Tongue* includes some pearls of wisdom I have acquired through my experience of hard knocks, much research, receiving help from mentors, and a good deal of trial and error. It will help you verbally communicate respect and kindness no matter the situation. Whether in the virtual sphere or personal encounters, the art of controlling one's tongue remains a potent force in fostering understanding, unity, and a more empathetic society.

While not intended as an academic treatment on the subject, provided references allow the studious to dig deeply into the research. The aim here is a practical one, and follows 4 basic steps:

**1. Know Yourself:** We will look at this from a few different perspectives, including a piece on neuroscience. The rationale in this section is relatively simple. Before you can improve, you need to know who you are.

**2. Heal Yourself:** Take ownership of the self-healing process by getting help when you need it. Everyone needs help to survive and grow at some stage in life. Once you become aware of what may cause you to speak rashly, healing can begin. You will learn how to uncover the causes and how to heal.

**3. Master Yourself:** Once you know yourself more fully and have healed to the extent possible, you reach the fun part—the practice of mindful speaking. In this part of the book, you choose practical exercises to make this process enjoyable and highly effective.

**4. Get Connected:** A mentor helped me when my tongue got me into trouble at work. This section concerns finding a mentor and several other important levels of connection. After all, communication is about connecting with people. Tips on how to optimize those connections are discussed. And finally, we suggest a way to stay mindful at all times—preparing you for opportunities when your spoken words can improve a moment in time.

# STEP ONE

## KNOW YOURSELF

*It helps to know what drives your tongue—the instincts, emotions, cognitions, and habits that become the words you say and how you say them. This is the first step. Remain curious and non-judgmental. To know what occurs within us as we speak is powerful. To become aware of this within yourself is transformative.*

# CHAPTER 1

## The Neuroscience of Emotion

**"You have power over your mind—not outside events. Realize this, and you will find strength."** —Marcus Aurelius

When you talk to people, your emotions play a big part in how you express yourself. It's like your feelings have a way of seeping into your words, tone, and even your body language. That's where neuroscience comes in. It helps you understand what's happening in your brain when you experience different emotions. It can help you understand why you feel the way you do and how it affects your communication.

Why is this important in mindful speaking? When you speak mindfully, you're not just focusing on picking the right words. You're also tuning in to the emotional vibe of the conversation. By understanding the neuroscience of emotion, you gain valuable insights into how your emotions shape the way you talk and interact with others. It's like having a roadmap that helps you navigate your emotions and use them to enhance your communication skills.

In this chapter, I invite you to take a close look at the fascinating connection between your brain and emotions. Together, we will explore the different parts of the brain, such as the amygdala and prefrontal cortex, and see how they play a role in processing your emotions. We'll also look at neurotransmitters and hormones to understand how these tiny molecules can impact your feelings. By the end of this chapter, you'll have a better understanding of how your emotions arise and are managed by your brain. You can then use this knowledge to improve the way you communicate with others.

## Understanding Emotions

Emotions are created by your mind based on your past experiences and, in some cases, your instinct. Like a high-speed supercomputer, your brain uses the memory of the past and instincts to predict what is most likely to happen next. You use this information to take action and make decisions.

You need emotions to make decisions. Strange as it may seem at first glance, your ability to decide is paralyzed without emotional input. Research shows individuals with damage to the parts of the brain that create and process emotions become incapable of making rational decisions. (Gupta, 2011) These main areas are the amygdala, which lie at the base of the brain, and the prefrontal cortex, located at the front.

Emotions are tied with memories and act like an internal compass that guides you through your experiences. They're complex reactions that can affect not only how you consciously feel but also how you behave and communicate with the world around you.

When you experience something, whether a joyful moment or challenging situation, your brain and body work together like a supercomputer to create your emotional response. It's a fascinating process that involves both physiological and cognitive elements.

On the physiological side, when you experience an emotion, your body reacts in specific ways. For example, if you are scared, your heart rate might increase, and you might sweat. These physical reactions are your body's way of preparing you to face the situation.

On the cognitive side, your brain plays a crucial role in processing the situation and interpreting it based on your past experiences, beliefs, and thoughts. This interpretation then influences how you feel and how you express that emotion. For instance, if you see a friend you haven't seen in a long time, your brain processes the situation and triggers feelings of happiness and excitement. This emotional response might make you smile, hold out your arms for a big hug and say, "I've missed you so much!"

Imagine you're walking in the park and see a cute puppy. Your brain processes the image of the puppy and thinks, "Oh, that's adorable!" This thought then triggers a feeling of happiness. Your body reacts by making you smile, and you might even say, "Aww, how cute!" in a happy tone. That's your emotional response in action.

In essence, emotions are a vital part of human experience. They influence not just your internal self but also how you interact with others. By understanding your emotions and the processes involved in creating them, you learn to navigate your emotions more effectively. This, in turn, can help you communicate mindfully and build stronger, more meaningful connections with the people around you.

## Understanding the Neural Circuits of Emotion

The neuroscience of emotion is fascinating and beautiful. Let's throw on our lab coats and peer through a microscope for a good look at what's happening inside our brains when we experience emotions.

By exploring the neural circuits, brain regions, and chemical messengers involved in emotion processing, we gain a deeper understanding of how our emotions work and how they affect our behavior and communication.

The creation and processing of emotions take place along our neurons—the wiring of the supercomputer-like organ we call the brain. But, unlike the wiring of a computer, our neurons are alive and capable of changing their wiring in dynamic ways. Further, they are affected by, and act upon, sensory input from our bodies and by numerous chemicals with which they come in contact.

## Hierarchical, Parallel Processing Streams, and Feedback Loops in Neural Circuits for Emotion

One of the key features of the neural circuits involved in emotion processing is the presence of hierarchical and parallel processing streams. Hierarchical processing means figuring things out by going through a series of steps in order. Parallel processing means making sense of something by taking in all the input at once.

An example of hierarchical processing in the practice of medicine is the evaluation of a patient with a fever of unknown origin. These are patients with a fever to 101 degrees Fahrenheit or more on most days, for at least 3 weeks, without a diagnosis despite a week of initial investigation. The evaluation proceeds stepwise, usually like this: 1) study the patient's history, including a list of their medications and supplements; 2) perform a head-to-toe physical exam; 3) undertake some lab work, including blood and urine cultures; 4) obtain a chest x-ray if not already done; 5) unless a cause is readily found during the above steps, obtain a CT scan of the chest, abdomen, and pelvis. The point is that the evaluation takes place in a stepwise manner. That step-by-step process is the essence of hierarchical processing.

An example of parallel processing in the emergency department could go like this: a young, tall, thin man is brought into the emergency department complaining of sudden onset of right-sided chest pain and shortness of breath while hunting. There was no trauma. He appears in distress, and the nurse reports a blood pressure of 80 over 60, a heart rate of 140 and an oxygen saturation of 80%.

When an emergency room doctor takes just a few seconds to make this diagnosis, they are engaged in parallel processing. The experienced doctor recognizes all this input instantly, by pattern recognition, without the need to go through a step-by-step analysis. A quick listen to the chest confirms the diagnosis. This patient has a tension pneumothorax, meaning a collapsed lung, and the resulting increased pressure on the heart and blood vessels is threatening the patient's life. The doctor inserts a 14-gauge needle into a precise location in the patient's chest, stabilizing them within minutes. A chest x-ray and the placement of a chest tube can now be performed with the patient in better shape.

As your brain generates and evaluates emotions, it does both hierarchical and parallel processing. These streams allow for the integration of information from different sources, such as sensory inputs, memory, and cognitive processes, to generate emotional responses.

The hierarchical organization of these circuits ensures information is processed in a step-by-step manner, with each level of processing adding complexity to the emotional response. Parallel processing streams, on the other hand, allow for the simultaneous processing of different aspects of an emotional stimulus, such as its valence—that is, whether it's good or bad, and its intensity.

Feedback loops are also crucial in emotion processing. Feedback loops are physiological mechanisms that play a vital role in maintaining homeostasis, the internal stability required for the proper functioning of the body. When considering emotions, the regulation of mood and emotional states involves a complex interplay of neural and hormonal feedback loops based on past experiences and contextual information. These feedback loops help to fine-tune emotional responses, ensuring they are appropriate to the situation at hand.

## Neural Circuits for Emotion Are Organized at Multiple Scales

The neural circuits for emotion are organized at multiple scales, ranging from microcircuits that involve small groups of neurons to macro circuits that extend to the large areas of the brain. This organization allows for the integration of information from different sources and the generation of coordinated emotional responses. It can also help us recover, to a remarkable degree, from trauma or disease.

At the microscale, individual neurons and small groups of neurons process specific aspects of an emotional stimulus, such as its valence or intensity. These microcircuits then feed into larger circuits that process all this information.

At the macroscale, large areas of the brain, such as the amygdala and prefrontal cortex, are involved in the processing of emotional stimuli. These areas of the brain ultimately generate the emotional response.

## The Amygdala and Emotional Processing

Nestled deep within your brain, the amygdala acts as a central hub for emotional processing, playing a pivotal role in deciphering the emotional significance of your surroundings. This almond-shaped structure meticulously sifts through a myriad of sensory inputs, assigning emotional values such as positivity or negativity, intensity, and even approachability to each stimulus. Located in the medial temporal lobe, it is integral to your experience of a range of emotions, from fear and pleasure to anger. It is near the brainstem, where the vagus nerve arises. Gut feelings reach the brainstem via the vagus nerve, and from transit there, the brainstem relays this information directly to the amygdala and nearby structures.

Beyond emotional processing, the amygdala is a key player in regulating automatic functions (like heartbeat and digestion) and hormonal balances, ensuring your body operates in harmony. It also aids in decision-making by weighing emotional responses and is a major factor in adapting your instinctive and motivational behaviors in response to environmental changes.

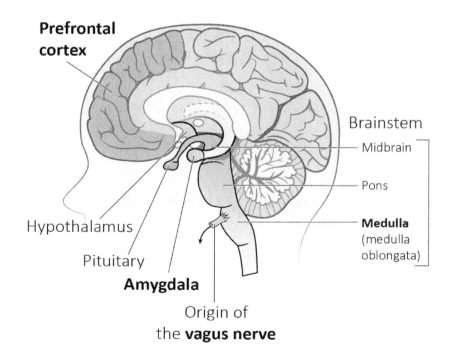

## The Role of the Amygdala in Emotional Learning

Implicit associative learning, a type of learning that occurs without conscious awareness, is facilitated by the amygdala. This process is crucial for the formation of emotional memories and the association of specific stimuli with emotional responses. The ability to remember things based on how you feel in response to something pre-dates your ability to think with words. This explains why you may have high blood pressure and sweaty palms when you visit the doctor or dentist, though you cannot remember why. Maybe as a baby, you were held down and received a shot or had a stick put in your mouth while some stranger (the doctor) looked inside your throat. You can't remember this verbally since you were just a baby. But deep in the center of your brain, the amygdala and the insula have it logged and instantly reveal it again when you face a similar situation. That is implicit associative learning.

The amygdala is also involved in changes in short- and long-term synaptic plasticity, essential for consolidating emotional memories.

## The Amygdala and the Fight-or-Flight Response

A key player in the activation of the fight-or-flight response, the amygdala responds to perceived threats by signaling for the release of stress hormones such as adrenaline and activating the sympathetic nervous system. This prepares the body to either confront or flee from the threat.

26

To understand how the nerves are communicating, you need to know some terminology. Nerve cells are also called "neurons." When we talk about how neurons send and receive signals, we use the terms "efferent" and "afferent" to inform you which direction the electrical current is flowing. So, current moving from the neuron to someplace else is called "efferent"—with an "e." Current coming from someplace else to a neuron we are referencing is called "afferent"—with an "a." Surface structures of the brain are called "cortical," while those that lie beneath the surface are "subcortical."

Efferent projections from the amygdala to cortical and subcortical structures, such as the hypothalamus and brainstem, initiate the fight-or-flight response.

## The Amygdala and Decision-Making

In decision-making processes, particularly involving emotional responses, the amygdala evaluates the emotional significance of stimuli and generates appropriate emotional responses. It also regulates instinctive and motivational behaviors essential for survival, such as feeding and mating. It's no coincidence that swear words often depict either digestion or mating.

It's important to understand your emotions are often created before you are consciously aware of them. This is based on previous experiences, DNA, and, in some cases, instinct. For example, you might instinctively withdraw from something that

27

resembles a snake. This demonstrates how deeply your emotions are intertwined with survival instincts and past experiences, influencing your decisions and actions, often before you even realize it.

## The Amygdala and Autonomic and Endocrine Functions

The amygdala plays a lead role in regulating autonomic and endocrine functions, vital for maintaining homeostasis in the body. The autonomic nervous system regulates involuntary functions like heart rate, blood pressure, and digestion, while the endocrine system controls various physiological processes through hormone release, such as metabolism, growth, and reproduction. The amygdala integrates sensory information and generates appropriate autonomic and endocrine responses to emotional stimuli.

## The Prefrontal Cortex and Emotional Processing

Situated at the front of the frontal lobe, the prefrontal cortex is integral to how you process emotions, aiding in the understanding and management of your emotional responses. This area enables you to evaluate different situations, make sense of your emotions, and respond appropriately to social and environmental stimuli.

A key function of the prefrontal cortex is regulating emotions and controlling emotional reactions. It assists in managing your feelings and responding to situations in a socially acceptable manner that benefits you. It is also involved in controlling impulsive behavior and making decisions aligned with your values and goals. Unfortunately, this area of the brain is readily impaired by alcohol.

## Decision-Making Processes

With decision-making, especially involving emotional responses, this area is key. It helps you weigh the pros and cons of different options, make informed decisions based on your emotional experiences, and predict the outcomes of your actions, understanding the consequences of your choices.

## Navigating Social Interactions

In social interactions, the prefrontal cortex is vital for interpreting social cues, such as facial expressions and body language, and responding appropriately to the emotions of others. This area is also involved in empathy, allowing you to understand and share the feelings of others.

## Memory Formation and Retrieval

Additionally, the prefrontal cortex contributes to forming and retrieving emotional memories, helping you remember past emotional experiences to guide your future behavior. It is also involved in consolidating long-term memories, ensuring your emotional experiences are stored and can be accessed when needed.

## Classic and Modern Examples

Scientific understanding of emotional control began by observing patients who endured various traumatic injuries, tumors, and seizure disorders.

The first classic case of these examples involved Phineas Gage, whose rock-blasting accident in 1848 severely damaged the left frontal lobe of his brain, causing him over five years of disabling loss of inhibition. (Teles, 2020; Van Horn, 2012). Prior to his injury, he was socially pleasant and known as a reliable worker. With the loss of inhibition from his accident, he cussed frequently and inappropriately, became rude and did not follow instructions. Despite this, Gage showed remarkable long-term recovery over the course of several years. He even improved enough to resume gainful employment driving carriages, a job that required restraint and judgment. He eventually developed seizures and retired to stay with relatives in San Francisco. He lived for 12 years after the accident, passing away in San Francisco in 1860.

More recent research shedding light on the neuroscience of emotion comes from functional MRI studies. Functional MRI takes advantage of the fact that iron holds oxygen in the center of hemoglobin molecules. Hemoglobin is what makes your blood red. And the iron at its center has different magnetic properties depending on how much oxygen it is carrying. The more oxygen going to a particular area of the brain, the more intense the MRI signal will be. Therefore, when a study volunteer undergoes a functional MRI and is exposed to emotion-triggering images or words, researchers can determine which areas of their brain are activated.

To me, one of the most inspiring of these MRI studies was done to understand the minds of those lucky enough to remain deeply in love with their partner for decades! How do they do it? What goes on in their minds? And how do they compare with couples who have recently fallen in love?

In New York around 2010 and 2011, ten women and seven men volunteered for the study. These volunteers were in long-term, deeply loving, monogamous relationships and were willing to be studied by functional MRI.

The researchers involved were an elite team: Bianca Acevedo and Arthur Aron from the Department of Psychology at Stony Brook, Helen Fisher from the Department of Anthropology at Rutgers, and Lucy Brown from the Department of Neurology at Albert Einstein College of Medicine. (Acevedo, 2012).

The selected study volunteers had responded to advertisements in New York City. To qualify, they had to pass a series of standard questionnaires validating their long-term relationships, and had to have no contraindication to undergoing MRI studies. Each study participant was required to provide facial photos of their partners, and of some friends and acquaintances.

Next, they were placed in MRI scanners, able to produce accurate images of the brain and to quickly detect changes in blood flow to different areas. The researchers looked for areas of the brain that experienced increased blood flow, indicating increased activity, as the participants were asked to rate how they felt about different photos they were shown. The ratings measured to what degree, if any, they felt a specific emotion as they saw each photo. Their responses to their partner's photo were then compared to their responses to photos of friends or acquaintances.

Positive emotions ran highest when shown photos of their partners, with the highest-scoring emotions being joy, love, and passion. Compared to activity when shown a friend or acquaintance, the MRI detected increased activity in the basal ganglia and the insula when they saw photos of their partner.

The ventrotegmental area, nestled between the substantia nigra in the midbrain, was the most active area associated with thoughts of loved ones. These regions of the brain are related to reward and pleasure. Dopamine is the primary neurotransmitter in play here. Other highly activated areas of the brain were those associated with maternal bonding, like the substantia nigra, globus pallidus, and the insula.

Acevedo and her colleagues published their findings in 2012, becoming the first to show the neuroanatomy of long-term, romantic love. Compared to studies of couples who had just recently fallen in love, these long-term lovers showed less activation in areas of the brain associated with anxiety and compulsivity. In a nutshell, the long-term lovers were much calmer.

You are not alone if the jealousy area of your brain is currently activated and firing like a rocket upon launch.

So yes, long-term, deep, passionate, bonding love does exist. At least, I would like to think it does. It will be especially encouraging should an unrelated group of researchers reproduce the findings from this study. Until then, we may feel that complex emotion expressed most accurately by the Portuguese word "saudade." And we can be thankful for those involved in researching the nature of emotion. Our understanding of this will undoubtedly advance as progress is made in the techniques and designs of research.

How does this relate to emotional regulation and mindful speaking? Well, when you talk to people, it's not just the words you use. Your emotions play a major part in how you communicate. That's why it's so important to understand and manage your emotions, especially when you want to have meaningful and effective conversations.

Think about when you were last furious or upset. Did your voice change? Maybe you spoke louder or faster, or your tone became sharper. That's because emotions influence the way you express yourself. When not in complete control of your emotions, your speech can become more negative or even harmful.

This is where emotional regulation comes in. Emotional regulation means an awareness of your emotions and managing them to communicate better. It's like taking a step back and saying, "Okay, I'm feeling really angry right now, but I'm going to take a deep breath and calm down before I say anything." By doing this, you can prevent misunderstandings and conflicts and have more positive interactions with other people.

Mindful speaking, on the other hand, involves being present and fully engaged in the conversation. It means really listening to the other person and thinking before you speak. When you practice mindful speaking, you are more likely to choose your words carefully and express yourself in a clearer and more respectful way. And when you combine mindful speaking with emotional regulation, you become a proficient speaker in any given social setting. Your communication shines with clarity and authenticity, engages your audience, and earns their respect.

# Wrapping Up: The Brain's Role in Emotions

The neural circuits involved in emotion processing are complex and involve multiple brain regions that work together to generate emotional responses. The hierarchical and parallel processing streams, feedback loops, and organization of neural circuits at multiple scales are extremely important for the integration of information from different sources and the generation of coordinated emotional responses.

The amygdala and the prefrontal cortex play central roles in the processing and regulation of emotions. The amygdala is involved in emotional learning, the fight-or-flight response, decision-making, and the regulation of autonomic and endocrine functions. It helps you to evaluate the emotional significance of stimuli and generate appropriate emotional responses. On the other hand, the prefrontal cortex is essential for regulating your emotions, controlling impulsive behavior, making informed decisions, and navigating social interactions. It helps you understand and manage your feelings, weigh the pros and cons of different options, and predict the outcomes of your actions. It is also integral to memory formation and retrieval, allowing you to learn from past experiences and use that knowledge to shape your future behavior.

With these insights, we are ready for the next chapter, where we will dive into the neuroscience of swearing.

# References:

Acevedo, B. P., Aron, A., Fisher, H. E., & Brown, L. L. (2012). Neural correlates of long-term intense romantic love. *Social cognitive and affective neuroscience*, *7*(2), 145–159. https://doi.org/10.1093/scan/nsq092

Gupta, R., Koscik, T. R., Bechara, A., & Tranel, D. (2011). The amygdala and decision-making. *Neuropsychologia*, *49*(4), 760–766. https://doi.org/10.1016/j.neuropsychologia.2010.09.029

Teles R. V. (2020). Phineas Gage's great legacy. *Dementia & neuropsychologia*, *14*(4), 419–421. https://doi.org/10.1590/1980-57642020dn14-040013

Van Horn, J. D., Irimia, A., Torgerson, C. M., Chambers, M. C., Kikinis, R., & Toga, A. W. (2012). Mapping connectivity damage in the case of Phineas Gage. *PloS one*, *7*(5), e37454. https://doi.org/10.1371/journal.pone.0037454

# CHAPTER 2

## The Neuroscience of Swearing

**"Better to light a candle than to curse the darkness."**
—ancient proverb

As I confessed in the introduction to this book, my previous tendency to cuss when frustrated nearly got me fired from work. Part of my response to this issue was to perform some research. While doing so, I ran across a case report published in the Journal of Epilepsy Research in 2021 about a 41-year-old man with seizures that caused him to swear. (Ju, 2021) This was first noticed at his workplace during the daily nap employees were allowed to take. Oddly, and out of character, the man began swearing out loud as he slept! His episodes began with stereotyped lip-smacking and repetitive arm movements, followed by swearing torrents that could quickly get a person fired.

Fortunately for our siesta-taking friend, neurologists were consulted. He was evaluated with an MRI, followed by continuous EEG and video monitoring as he slept. They found that his seizure activity began in the left temporal lobe of his brain. He responded well to anti-seizure medication. In his case, the medication used was oxcarbazepine, and voila! No more seizures or profanity outbursts!

There are variations in the neuroanatomy in other reported cases. Some involved the medial prefrontal cortex and the right temporal lobe. The term for these events of swearing caused by seizures is "ictal swearing."

In some cases, it can be controlled with medications, whereas others require surgery. At least our friend can rest easy, and thanks to him, we understand more about the neuroanatomy of swearing.

On that note, while it's commonly seen as rude or unrefined, it actually involves a complex interplay of brain regions and processes. In some workplaces, it is allowed—even encouraged. In others, though, like mine, it could cost you dearly.

In this chapter, we'll demystify the neuroscience behind swearing in simple terms to understand why it happens and what it does to us.

# The Brain's Language Network and Swearing

Swearing is a distinctive type of language, and it's deeply rooted in our brain's neural circuits. To decode how swearing operates neurologically, you should be aware of Broca's area, The Inferior Frontal Gyrus, and the Posterior Middle Temporal Gyrus—a few of the main anatomic areas involved. Broca's area is actually in the Inferior frontal gyrus, and both these areas are in the frontal lobe. The posterior middle temporal gyrus is on each side of the brain, slightly deep to the ear. Of course, other areas are in on it, such as the ventromedial prefrontal cortex— but more about that later.

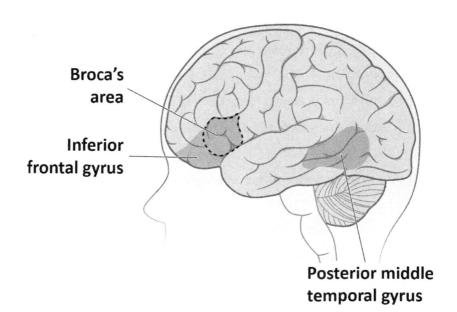

Broca's area

Inferior frontal gyrus

Posterior middle temporal gyrus

Situated in the frontal lobe, Broca's area is the brain's speech production center. Located on the dominant side of the brain (left side in a right-handed person), it's where the conversion of thoughts into words and sentences normally occurs. Interestingly, people who have lost the ability to speak due to damage to Broca's area can utter taboo or swear words when emotionally triggered. Similar responses with crude vocalizations and gestures are present in non-human primates such as chimpanzees.

In some situations, the use of taboo words is helpful, but a delicate subject, nonetheless. Given the proper context, swearing can improve bonding among co-workers, and repeated studies have shown that, used sparingly, it increases pain tolerance. (Byrne, 2017). Again, when used appropriately, it can improve the believability that what a person is saying is both important and trustworthy. (Byrne, 2017). Used inappropriately, however, swearing can lead to embarrassment, damaged relationships, job loss, and, in some cultures, severe legal penalties. These words are labelled "taboo" for a reason.

So how do you—or your mind—determine when, if ever, to speak taboo words? This is an area of ongoing research, but anatomically, at least, the "filter" occurs prominently within two well-defined areas of the brain: a part of the temporal lobe called the posterior middle temporal gyrus and the Inferior frontal gyrus. High levels of activity were found in these areas using functional MRI studies while subjects were asked to quickly name out loud a series of images they were shown. However, next to each image were unrelated, distracting words. When shown an image with a taboo distracting word, they slowed their verbal response. During that pause, the MRI showed increased activity in those two areas of the brain mentioned: the Inferior frontal gyrus and the posterior middle temporal gyrus. (Hansen, 2019).

When we're compelled to swear, whether in frustration or surprise, it's Broca's area that springs into action. This region coordinates the muscles in the jaw, lips, and tongue to produce the distinct swear words. It's almost like a reflex; these words can come out without the filtering process that non-swear words typically undergo.

## Wernicke's Area: The Hub of Language Comprehension

Wernicke's area, located in the temporal lobe, just superior to the posterior middle temporal gyrus, is essential for understanding both spoken and written language. It's the brain's language interpreter. When we hear someone swear, Wernicke's area processes not just the words but also the emotional charge they carry. This area enables us to perceive whether the words are meant to harm, joke, or express pain, making it a critical component in interpreting the full spectrum of communication.

## The Emotional Dimension of Swearing

While Broca's and Wernicke's areas handle the linguistic structure and comprehension of swearing, the emotional weight of swear words engages other brain regions. The limbic system, particularly the amygdala, lights up when we swear, linking our emotional state to the words we choose. This connection explains why swearing often accompanies emotional extremes, such as frustration, anger, or pain. The amygdala's involvement suggests that swear words are not just linguistic expressions but also emotional ones, serving as an outlet for intense feelings.

## The Integrated Network of Swearing

Swearing is not an isolated function; it's a complex, integrated process. When we swear, we're not just using Broca's and Wernicke's area; we're also engaging the basal ganglia, which play a role in the automaticity of well-learned behaviors, including the habitual use of swear words. Additionally, the prefrontal cortex is involved in the social aspect of swearing, such as deciding when it's appropriate to use such language and understanding the potential impact on listeners.

In summary, swearing is a multifaceted neurological event that involves language production, comprehension, and emotional expression. It's a testament to the complexity of human communication and the intricate workings of our brain's language network. Understanding these neural underpinnings can shed light on why swearing is a universal yet powerful part of human language.

# Emotional Processing and Swearing

Swearing is intricately linked to our emotional processes, especially in situations of stress, anxiety, and depression. It often serves as an unfiltered outlet for intense feelings, and the amygdala's role is pivotal in this expressive phenomenon.

## The Amygdala: Emotional Trigger for Swearing

When we encounter a startling, painful, or infuriating situation, the amygdala reacts almost instantaneously, like an emotional alarm system. This reaction can trigger a cascade of responses, including the release of stress hormones and an increase in heart rate, preparing the body for a fight-or-flight response.

In the context of swearing, the amygdala's activation can lead to the spontaneous exclamation of swear words. It's as if the emotional intensity overflows into our speech, bypassing the usual social and linguistic filters. Swearing can thus be seen as a primal and immediate form of emotional expression.

## The Limbic System: The Emotional Network's Role in Swearing

The limbic system, which encompasses the amygdala, is often

referred to as the emotional brain. It's a network that not only processes our feelings but also influences our behavior and long-term memory. This system's interconnection with the brain's language-producing regions means our speech is imbued with emotional resonance.

When we swear, we're tapping into this deep-seated emotional network. The limbic system's involvement in swearing is evident in the way our voice might change pitch, volume, or intensity when we use expletives. This is not just a linguistic pattern but an emotional one, revealing the underlying feelings the words represent.

## The Role of the Prefrontal Cortex in Regulating Swearing

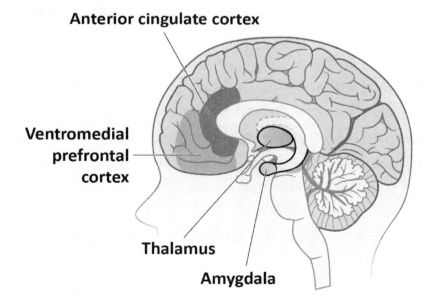

While the amygdala and the limbic system initiate the emotional impetus to swear, the prefrontal cortex is responsible for moderating this impulse. This part of the brain is involved in decision-making, social behavior, and the inhibition of inappropriate reactions. (This is the area damaged in the case of Phineas Gage, the man injured while blasting rock to clear a path for the Rutland & Burlington Railroad in 1848). When you choose not to swear, even when emotionally aroused, your prefrontal cortex is exercising its regulatory function.

However, when the emotional response is strong enough, or when the prefrontal cortex's inhibitory mechanisms are not fully engaged, such as during periods of stress, anger, or after consuming alcohol, swearing is more likely to occur. The prefrontal cortex's role in emotional regulation and impulse control is crucial in understanding why we might swear in some situations and hold back in others.

## The Integration of Emotion and Language in Swearing

The act of swearing is a complex interplay between our emotional brain and our language centers. It's a demonstration of how tightly woven our emotions are with our communicative expressions. Swearing can serve as a pressure valve, releasing emotional tension through language. This release can be cathartic, providing a sense of relief as the emotional energy is given voice.

In essence, the neuroscience behind swearing reveals not merely a linguistic or social phenomenon but a deeply rooted emotional response. By understanding the brain structures involved in emotional processing and their connection to language, we can appreciate the powerful role that swearing plays in human expression and communication.

## Swearing and the Autonomic Nervous System

Swearing doesn't just happen in the brain; it affects the whole body. The autonomic nervous system, which controls our involuntary actions like heartbeat and breathing, responds to swearing. For example, if you swear when you're angry, you might notice your heart rate speeds up. This response is controlled by the hypothalamus, an area of the brain that works with the autonomic nervous system to prepare the body for a quick reaction, like fight or flight.

## Pain and Swearing

Have you noticed that you might swear when you hurt yourself? This isn't just a social habit; it's rooted in our brain's response to pain. Swearing can actually help us tolerate pain better. (Byrne, 2017). This is because it triggers a stress response that can reduce the feeling of pain. The somatosensory cortex, a part of the brain that processes sensory information like touch and pain, is less responsive when we use swear words. This means that swearing can provide a temporary relief from discomfort.

## Swearing and Social Cognition

The decision to swear or not in social situations involves the prefrontal cortex, the part of the brain behind your forehead. This area is responsible for decision-making, understanding social norms, and self-control. When you choose to swear, your prefrontal cortex is weighing the social context, your emotions, and the potential consequences of your words.

## Swearing, Stress, and the Brain

Swearing is also related to stress. When we're stressed, our body releases hormones like cortisol. The brain has a system for managing our stress response, known as the HPA axis, which involves the hypothalamus, pituitary gland, and adrenal glands. Swearing can sometimes act as a release valve for stress, lowering cortisol levels and make us feel less tense.

## Neurological Disorders and Swearing

In some neurological disorders, such as Tourette syndrome, people may swear involuntarily. This is because of disruptions in the basal ganglia, a group of structures in the brain that help control movement and speech. These disruptions can lead to tics, which are sudden, repetitive movements or sounds that can include swearing.

## Ancient Roots of Swearing

Swearing serves as a way to express strong emotions without physical confrontation. And it's not just us humans who do this. Chimpanzees and other primates use emotionally charged vocal and physical gestures for some of the same reasons humans do. We share the use of taboo expression as a non-violent way to warn intruders, assert dominance, or express anger.

## The Cognitive Benefits of Swearing

Despite its stigma, swearing can have some cognitive benefits. It can signify a rich vocabulary and strong language skills. Engaging in swearing activates the dorsolateral prefrontal cortex, an area involved in complex tasks like planning and problem-solving. This suggests that swearing can be part of a dynamic and effective use of language.

## Swearing and Mindful Speaking: Balancing Expression and Composure

As we navigate the intricate pathways of our brain's response to emotions, we encounter the spontaneous and often cathartic act of swearing. Yet, in the realm of mindful speaking, where does this natural impulse fit?

## Understanding the Impulse to Swear

Swearing can be an instinctive emotional response, a release valve for the intense pressure of bottled-up feelings. It's a primal language that often bypasses our social filters, providing a raw, unadulterated expression of our inner state. However, when we aim to engage in mindful speaking, we're faced with the challenge of harnessing this impulse, transforming it into something that aligns with our intentions and the context of our interactions.

## Emotional Regulation: The Key to Mindful Swearing

The art of mindful speaking doesn't necessarily exclude swearing; rather, it involves the conscious regulation of our emotional responses. Emotional regulation is the process of recognizing our feelings, understanding their origins, and deciding how to express them in a way that serves our communication goals. It's finding the right balance between expressing authenticity and maintaining a sense of decorum.

Sometimes, to achieve this requires some inner healing, which we will explore later. And for some, such as people with post-traumatic stress disorder, complete conscious regulation may not be a reasonable goal—at least not until research leads to additional clinical breakthroughs.

## Swearing with Intention: A Mindful Approach

When used intentionally and sparingly, swearing can add emphasis and convey the depth of our feelings without derailing a conversation. It's the difference between a well-placed expletive that highlights our passion and a barrage that obscures our message. Mindful swearing is about using such language as a rhetorical tool, not as a habitual reaction. And a word to the wise: never use religious or racial slurs. That can make enemies fast. While swearing can momentarily alleviate stress or pain, it's essential to consider its impact on our listeners. In some contexts, swearing can strengthen bonds and signal openness, while in others, it can offend or create distance. Mindful speaking involves gauging the social landscape and adapting our language to foster connection and understanding.

## Cultivating Mindful Speaking Habits

To cultivate the habit of mindful speaking, practice pausing before reacting, choosing your words with care, and reflecting on the potential effects of your language. This doesn't mean suppressing your emotions but rather expressing them in a way that's both true to yourself and considerate of others.

# Wrapping Up

Swearing is a complex linguistic phenomenon that involves various brain regions and processes. It's intertwined with your emotions, social interactions, and even your body's stress responses. Understanding the neuroscience behind swearing gives you insight into not just why you might swear, but also the broader capabilities and adaptability of your language and brain.

By examining swearing from a neurological perspective, you can appreciate its role in human communication and its potential benefits. As you continue to explore the art and science of mindful speaking, this knowledge can help you make more informed choices about how you use language in your daily life.

Having explored the neuroscience of swearing, we'll now look at how it affects habits, and how you can learn and unlearn behaviors through conscious effort.

# References:

Byrne, E. (2017). Swearing is go*d f*r you: the amaz!ng sc!ence of bad language. Profile Books.

Hansen SJ, McMahon KL, de Zubicaray GI. The neurobiology of taboo language processing: fMRI evidence during spoken word production. Soc Cogn Affect Neurosci. 2019 Mar 5;14(3):271-279. doi: 10.1093/scan/nsz009. PMID: 30715549; PMCID: PMC6399611.

Teles R. V. (2020). Phineas Gage's great legacy. *Dementia & neuropsychologia*, *14*(4), 419–421. https://doi.org/10.1590/1980-57642020dn14-040013

Van Horn, J. D., Irimia, A., Torgerson, C. M., Chambers, M. C., Kikinis, R., & Toga, A. W. (2012). Mapping connectivity damage in the case of Phineas Gage. *PloS one*, *7*(5), e37454. https://doi.org/10.1371/journal.pone.0037454

# CHAPTER 3

## The Neuroscience of Habit Change

**"If you want to do something, make a habit of it."** —Epictetus

In the art of communication, your spoken words are most powerful. Yet, it's your habits that dictate the flow of those words, for better or worse. This chapter builds upon emotions and the automatic verbal expression of those emotions. You can use what you learned to shape your habits towards your goal of mindful speaking. As with emotions, understanding habits begins in the deepest areas of the brain—the basal ganglia.

# The Basal Ganglia: The Seat of Habit Formation

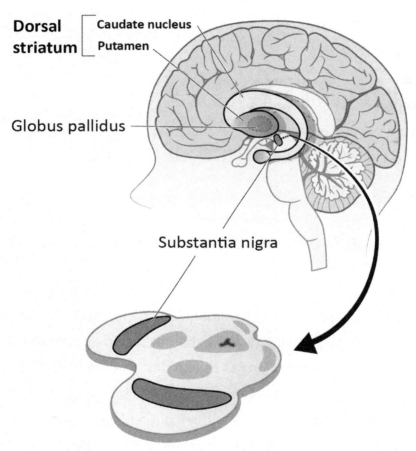

Slice of the midbrain

The basal ganglia are a cluster of nuclei, or neuron cell bodies, located deep within the cerebral hemispheres of the brain. Along with the cerebellum, they play a pivotal role in coordinating motor control, but are also integral to the process of habit formation. When you repeat a behavior frequently, the basal ganglia establish a pattern you can activate with minimal conscious thought. By doing this, your mind is freed from having to think through every little step involved in everything you do, from saying "Good morning" to driving a car, and whatever skilled task you have to complete on a moment's notice. This is because the basal ganglia are involved in the reinforcement of the association between a specific context or stimulus and the action that follows. Over time, this reinforcement makes the response more automatic.

## Procedural Memory: How Habits are Encoded in the Brain

Procedural memory is a form of long-term memory that allows you to carry out tasks without deliberate thought. It's the memory segment that stores your habits. In contrast to declarative memory, which is concerned with the recall of information and occurrences, procedural memory deals with the methodologies of activities.

Activities such as riding a bicycle, typing, or even speaking certain phrases in conversation are stored in procedural memory. The encoding of habits into procedural memory involves the repetition of actions, leading to increased efficiency in the neural pathways responsible for those actions, effectively embedding the habit into your neural circuitry.

# The Cycle of Habit Formation: Cue, Routine, Reward Demystified

The cycle of habit formation is a framework that delineates the anatomy of habits through a tripartite sequence:

**Cue:** This element acts as a signal that prompts the brain to switch to autopilot and select an appropriate habit to enact. It might be a particular place, a time of day, an emotional state, the company of certain individuals, or a recently occurred action.

**Routine:** The actual habitual action, which can manifest as a physical, mental, or emotional activity. In the sphere of habitual speech, for example, the routine could involve the use of specific expressions in response to inquiries or while offering feedback.

**Reward:** The reward serves as the brain's way of determining whether this specific habit cycle is worth embedding into future behavior. It is the positive feedback that comes after the routine, such as a feeling of contentment, a sense of achievement, or a moment of relief.

With repetition, this cycle — cue, routine, reward — solidifies into a more automatic sequence, where the cue and the reward become closely linked, fostering a strong sense of anticipation and craving. This dynamic is what underlies the formation of habitual behaviors, including speech-related habits. Grasping this cycle is pivotal for altering detrimental habits or cultivating new, constructive ones.

# The Neurobiology of Habit Formation

Habitual behaviors are actions we perform automatically, often without conscious thought. These behaviors are supported by neural pathways—the connections between neurons in the brain strengthened through repetition. When we first try to learn a new behavior, our prefrontal cortex, involved in planning and decision-making, is highly active.

As we repeat the behavior, the activity begins to shift to the basal ganglia, where habits are formed. This shift allows the behavior to become more automatic and efficient, requiring less energy and cognitive effort, which is why habits are so powerful; they enable us to conserve mental resources.

## Dopamine and the Reward System: Fueling Habit Formation

Dopamine is a neurotransmitter that is a major factor in the brain's reward system. It is released in response to pleasurable activities, but it also reinforces the desire to repeat behaviors that lead to those pleasures. When a behavior is associated with a reward, dopamine signals that the action is worth remembering and repeating. This release of dopamine strengthens the neural pathways associated with the behavior, making it more likely to become a habit. Over time, the cue's presence alone can trigger the release of dopamine, even before the reward is achieved, further solidifying the habit loop.

### The Role of the Striatum in Habit Automation

The striatum is a component of the basal ganglia and plays a critical role in habit automation. It receives input from various regions of the brain, including the cortex, and processes this information to help coordinate the appropriate responses. The striatum is particularly important for the formation of habits because it is where the initial learning of the behavior takes place. As the behavior is repeated, the striatum becomes more efficient at activating the habit, eventually making the behavior automatic. This process is known as habituation, allowing the brain to perform the behavior with less effort and more reliability. The striatum, therefore, acts as a central hub for the automation of behaviors repeated over time.

# The Role of Neurotransmitters in Habit Persistence and Change

Decades of research prove that many of our habits are unconscious, and the prefrontal cortex switches off, putting us on autopilot. One example is checking your phone excessively for messages or notifications. Such habits cause the brain to release dopamine, often recognized for its role in the brain's reward system, but its functions extend much further.

## Dopamine: Beyond Reward to Motivation and Learning

Dopamine extends to motivation and learning, critical for habit persistence and change. When you perform an action that satisfies a need or desire, dopamine is released, reinforcing the behavior, encouraging you to repeat it in the future. With habit formation, dopamine strengthens the neural pathways associated with the rewarding behavior, making it easier to activate. For habit change, dopamine's role in motivation is key. It reinforces the learning of new behaviors as you begin to associate them with positive outcomes or rewards.

More about temperance later, but this is a good time to point out that "mind-altering substances," such as alcohol, opiates, cocaine, and methamphetamine, stimulate the release of dopamine in the pleasure and habit-forming areas of the brain. Simultaneously, they impair the function of the prefrontal cortex. Their use rewards further use, and frequent use damages the part of the brain you need to master the art of mindful speaking.  If you struggle with this, you are not alone. I have treated people from all walks of life for addiction issues, including fellow doctors and allied healthcare workers. Professional help is indicated for those who find they cannot stop feeding harmful materials into their body.

As you seek to learn a new skill, periodic rewards positively engage this dopamine effect to shape your habits in the desired direction. For example, if you want to develop the new habit of pausing before you speak, you might begin with this: in the privacy of your own home, practice taking a slow, deep breath before responding to a verbally aggressive person. You could even role-play the other person's verbal aggression in a mirror before you then take that slow, deep breath. The successful practice of this is itself a reward. You could even take this up a notch by putting money in a "well-done-you" jar each time you practice, then reward yourself with a spending spree once you have practiced it enough.

## Serotonin and Mood: Their Influence on Habitual Behavior

Serotonin is a chemical messenger in the brain often associated with promoting happiness and well-being. It helps control mood, hunger, and sleep patterns, which can affect routine behaviors. Low levels of serotonin are associated with depression and can decrease motivation, making it harder to form new habits or break old ones.

Conversely, when serotonin levels are normal or enhanced, an individual may have a more positive outlook, increasing the willingness to engage in new, healthier habits. This is why activities that increase serotonin levels, such as exercise or exposure to sunlight, can be beneficial for habit change.

## Acetylcholine and Attention: Focusing on New Habits

Acetylcholine is involved in the modulation of attention and arousal and boosts learning and memory. When it comes to habits, the ability to focus on a new behavior is essential for its formation. Acetylcholine helps to direct attention to new tasks and can enhance sensory perception, indispensable when learning new behavior patterns. To optimize your acetylcholine levels, ensure you get enough rest, choose healthy foods, and regularly exercise both mind and body. By increasing your acetylcholine levels, you are putting yourself in the best position to improve your concentration. This focused attention is necessary to override existing habits and to encode new behaviors into procedural memory.

# Neuroplasticity and Habit Change

Neuroplasticity refers to the brain's ability to reorganize itself by forming new neural connections throughout life in response to intrinsic or extrinsic stimuli. Neuroplasticity might occur after a traumatic brain injury or learning a new skill such as playing the guitar. How does neuroplasticity change habits?

## The Brain's Adaptability: Learning and Unlearning Habits

The brain's ability to adapt is fundamental to learning new behaviors and unlearning old ones, including habits. When you attempt to change a habit, you are essentially asking your brain to break down old connections and build new ones. This process involves weakening the neural pathways that underlie the old habit and strengthening the pathways for the new behavior. The brain's plastic nature means that, although habits can be deeply ingrained, they are not permanent and can be altered with consistent effort and repetition.

## Synaptic Plasticity: Strengthening New Connections for New Habits

Synaptic plasticity is the ability of synapses, the points where neurons connect and communicate, to strengthen or weaken over time in response to increases or decreases in their activity. When we practice a new habit, the synapses involved in these behaviors become more efficient at transmitting signals. This synaptic strengthening is what helps to solidify new habits. Each time the new behavior is repeated, the synaptic connections that support this behavior are reinforced. This is why repetition is so important in habit formation; it leverages synaptic plasticity to make the new behavior automatic and natural.

## The Role of Myelination in Speeding Up New Habit Formation

Myelination is the process by which myelin, a fatty substance, accumulates around nerve fibers. This sheath acts as insulation and allows electrical impulses to travel along the nerve cells quickly and efficiently. When forming new habits, myelination speeds up the transmission of neural signals associated with the new behavior. As a habit becomes more established through practice, the relevant neural pathways become more myelinated, allowing for faster and more efficient communication between neurons. This increased speed and efficiency make the new habit easier to perform and more resistant to disruption. It becomes automatic.

# Neuroscience of Habit Change in Mindful Speaking

Mindful speaking requires altering the ingrained speech patterns deeply embedded in our neural circuitry. The process begins with the recognition of the automatic nature of our current speaking habits. The basal ganglia, which play a key role in the formation of habits, are responsible for the automaticity of these speech patterns. To change them, you must engage the prefrontal cortex, the area of the brain that governs conscious thought and decision-making. That area is inhibited by alcohol and impaired by concussions, both of which should be avoided to maintain brain health.

## Strengthening the Mindful Speaking Loop

Creating a new 'mindful speaking loop' involves intentional practice. When you catch yourself before cussing and instead pause, take a deep breath, and choose a more thoughtful response, you engage in a new routine. This new routine, when repeated, can be reinforced by the rewarding feeling of having communicated effectively. Over time, this reward helps to solidify the new speaking habit.

## The Impact of Neuroplasticity on Speech Habits

As mentioned above, neuroplasticity refers to the brain's capacity to create and rearrange connections between neurons, particularly as a reaction to learning or new experiences. It serves as the bedrock for developing the practice of mindful speaking. Through regular engagement in mindful speaking, you harness the power of neuroplasticity to establish newer, better speaking patterns. You develop fresh neural routes that support the deliberate pause-and-reply habit of mindful speaking.

You can choose what that pause looks like. I take a deep breath and think of a pearl. A pearl represents how an irritation can be turned into a beautiful gem. Others take a deep breath and imagine the three gates mentioned by the poet Rumi: "Before you speak, let your words pass through three gates: Is it true? Is it necessary? Is it kind?"

## Dopamine: Reinforcing Mindful Speaking

Dopamine strongly influences habit formation by signaling a reward to the brain. When you experience positive outcomes from mindful speaking, such as being better understood or creating a more positive interaction, your brain releases dopamine. This release acts as a natural reward, reinforcing the new habit of speaking mindfully and motivating you to continue practicing it.

### Resisting Stress: Triggered Speech Habits

Stress can trigger a fallback to your default, less mindful way of speaking. Understanding the neuroscience of stress and habit can help you develop strategies to maintain mindful speaking under pressure. Techniques that reduce stress and engage the prefrontal cortex, such as deep breathing or mindfulness meditation, can help you maintain a state conducive to mindful speaking, even in stressful situations.

### Consolidating Mindful Speaking Habits

Consolidating new speaking habits is a gradual process that requires consistent practice. Each time you choose to speak mindfully, you reinforce the neural pathways associated with this behavior. With repeated practice, these pathways become stronger, making mindful speaking an automatic response. This is the essence of changing speech habits through the lens of neuroscience—it's a deliberate, practiced change in your brain's wiring supporting your goal of mindful communication.

# Wrapping Up

The neuroscience exploration of habit change underscores a profound truth about the human brain: it is designed for adaptation and growth. The mechanisms of neuroplasticity, synaptic plasticity, and neurotransmitter activity not only explain how habits form but also how they can be remolded. As you apply these principles to mindful speaking, you recognize the neural architecture in your head does not condemn you to repeat past mistakes; rather, it provides a scaffold for building new, more constructive habits.

This chapter has equipped you with an understanding that mindful speaking is not just an aspiration but a neurologically attainable goal, one you can reach through awareness, practice, the brain's innate ability to adapt, and a shiny new "well-done-you" jar.

I gave a few examples of mindfulness speaking exercises to try, and we will look at several more later. But first, we'll move on to gut feelings, and how they affect what you say and how you say it.

# CHAPTER 4

## The Gut-Brain-Throat Connection

**"A poem ... begins as a lump in the throat...."** —Robert Frost, in a letter to a literary critic, January 1, 1916.

Ever felt a lump in your throat just before you stood up to address a room full of people? Or before asking your boss for a raise? Maybe your voice "cracked" or lacked its usual mellow resonance when you spoke? In these same situations, do you experience butterflies in your stomach, a sudden loss of appetite, or maybe even nausea? If so, you are not alone!

In the vast majority of cases, there is nothing wrong with the throat. The feeling usually arises from the "fight-or-flight response." This is the sympathetic nervous system kicking in.

It works like this: you sense a threatening situation, consciously or unconsciously. Any or all of your five senses are at play here. They send this information to your amygdala. Based on instinct or previous experience, these sensations alert your amygdala to danger.

Unless this amygdala stimulation is calmed by input from the prefrontal cortex, a rapid cascade is triggered, amplifying the effect at each step. The amygdala alerts the hypothalamus to secrete corticotropin-releasing hormone (CRH), which stimulates the pituitary to secrete ACTH (adrenocorticotropic hormone), which stimulates the adrenal glands to secrete adrenaline. (Góralczyk-Bin´kowska, 2022). That adrenaline speeds up your heart, makes you breathe quickly, increases muscle tone in the throat, dries secretions in the voice box, and can even make it difficult to swallow. And voila! Guess what? You feel a lump in your throat!

Sometimes, the feeling of a lump in your throat or butterflies in your stomach is a good thing. It alerts you that something of emotional impact is happening. On the other hand, it can interfere with your ability to speak. So, what can you do about it?

## The Gut-Brain-Throat Axis

This is where the gut-brain-throat axis comes in. For one, breathing is automatic, but you can consciously slow it down and take a deep breath or two. As a result, you calm the fight-or-flight response by directly engaging the most interesting nerve in the body— the vagus nerve. (De Couck, 2019; Magnon, 2021). We will look at other mind-gut connections, but first—the vagus nerve.

# The Vagus Nerve

Arising from the medulla oblongata at the base of the brain, there are two vagus nerves—a right and left. Each side wanders to more places in the body than any other nerve. It is this fact that led to its name, "vagus," derived from the Latin root from which we get the word "vagabond." This so-called vagabond of a nerve receives sensory input from the eardrums, the back of the tongue and throat, and the voice box— otherwise known as the larynx, the esophagus, heart, lungs, stomach, small and large intestines, spleen, liver, and pancreas! That is one long and wandering nerve! Some might call it the trespasser of all trespassers.

How your ears and throat feel, and your ability to swallow and control your vocal cords depend upon the vagus nerve. As interconnected as this nerve is, emotions can affect muscle tension in the throat area (both the voice box and the swallowing muscles), and they transmit sensations from this area back up to the brain. If intense emotions or increased sensitivity of the nerves in the throat occur, guess what you feel: a lump sensation! This can lead to increased anxiety, causing further tension and even sensitivity in a feedback loop that leads to a panic attack.

Conversely, with awareness and practice, these sensations can trigger you to pause, take a deep breath, and notice what emotions and thoughts are associated with these feelings. With awareness and practice, you will learn to enjoy the process as you find and express your authentic, passionate voice. You just might find that when you feel that lump in your throat or those flutters in your gut, you remember to take a slow, deep breath, take stock of your emotions, and then give voice to some of the most prominent words ever spoken! Like Robert Frost said, "A poem begins ... with a lump in the throat."

That awareness – that intuitive gut feeling – is in large part communicated to the brain from the gut and throat by the vagus nerve. 80% of the information along the vagus nerve travels from the body back to the brain to let it know what is going on in those areas. The remaining 20% of nerve traffic is sending information to move the vocal cords, slow the heart and respiratory rate, and make it easier to swallow and digest your food. (Bonaz, 2018).

# The Course of the Vagus Nerve

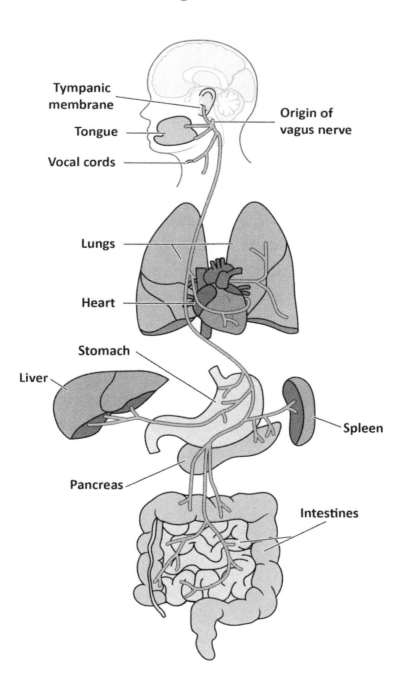

Tympanic membrane

Tongue

Vocal cords

Origin of vagus nerve

Lungs

Heart

Stomach

Liver

Spleen

Pancreas

Intestines

The vagus nerve is the dominant player of the parasympathetic nervous system, along with the nerves lining our intestines— the so-called enteric nervous system, or "ENS" for short. When the vagus and ENS are active in concert, you find it easier to remain calm and digest your food. This is why the parasympathetic nervous system is called the "rest and digest" part of the autonomic nervous system. In contrast, the sympathetic nervous system, with its amygdala-hypothalamus-pituitary-adrenal cascade, is called the "fight or flight" part of our autonomic nervous system. Input from both the parasympathetic and sympathetic nerves in our gut ultimately reaches your conscious awareness in the part of the brain called the insula. Interestingly, the insula also takes this input from your autonomic nervous system and includes it in your sense of risk versus reward. In this way, your gut feelings, processed in the insula, have much to do with the probability that you will repeat a specific action—including the action of a verbal response. Awareness of gut sensation resides in the insula, which includes those "gut feelings" to evaluate risk versus reward.

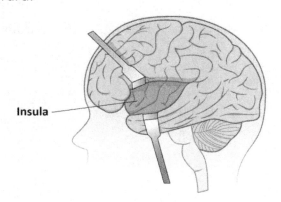

Insula

So you can calm yourself, make it easier to speak and swallow, and feel less of a lump in your throat by consciously taking a slow, deep breath. When you do that, you are stimulating the parasympathetic nervous system. (Breit, 2018). With practice in the form of meditation, yoga, swimming, or singing, you can master this. And that translates to more effective speaking.

Experiment with different means of calming yourself. Biofeedback is one method that is effective and fun, but it can be expensive. In my case, I initially tried meditation at the suggestion of a trusted mentor. I found meditation helpful, and still practice it sometimes. However, swimming works best for me. When you swim, you must be aware of and control your breathing. When I swim, I learn to stay relaxed even if the environment is uncomfortable. Sometimes, the water is on the chilly side. But I must stay relaxed, even if I'm swimming among icebergs, or I will use oxygen too quickly. Best of all, I am deliciously separate from my cell phone.

So, there you have the vagus nerve. And the insula. But what do the bacteria in your gut have to do with any of this?

## The Microscopic Organisms Inside Our Gut

Well, for one thing, a little perspective on our microbiome is in order. The microscopic organisms inside our guts, primarily bacteria, are too numerous to count—trillions in fact in any one human. More bacteria live in your gut than humans roam the planet! Those bacteria metabolize what you eat and make chemical byproducts, with many activating your body's immune and nervous systems. And since you have trillions of bacteria producing all sorts of byproducts of their own, many of these byproducts are absorbed into your bloodstream. When reviewing the data on this topic, by my calculation, 44% of the chemicals circulating in our blood come from these bacteria! (Diener, 2022).

Some of these chemicals, also called metabolites, stimulate your immune system, and can lead to an increase or a calming of inflammation in your gut and bloodstream. Some stimulate the hormone-producing cells in your gut, while others directly or indirectly stimulate the vagus nerve, letting your brain know how your gut is feeling. (Mayer, 2022).

And this communication from the microbes in the gut to the brain goes both ways. For example, if you are feeling stressed, the amygdala in your brain will set off a cascade of events that leads to increased adrenaline and cortisol in your circulation. Cortisol suppresses immunity, which can cause a leaky gut and an imbalance of the bacteria residing there.

Besides stress, what you regularly eat and drink affects which bacteria thrive in your gut and which do not. This effect is most significant in the first few years of life but is still important at any age. My review of various international research teams has shown that the best diet to maintain a healthy gut microbiome is simple: eat a variety of unprocessed foods, including plenty of vegetables. Include some healthy fats like avocado, olives, nuts, or fish that swim in cold water, such as mackerel, salmon, and sardines, as they are better for your gut and brain. And one more thing: include fermented foods like unsweetened yogurt, kefir, sauerkraut, kimchi, aged cheese, or miso. Some fermented foods may appeal to you, and some may disgust you. Try to find at least two you like and that help you feel better after eating them.

Despite the simple nutritional advice, its impact is critically important if you are to optimize your emotional health, as it will affect your speech.

An unfavorable change in the proportion of different types of bacteria in your gut can do more than make you irritable. It can lead to mental illness. Several studies have suggested it is a significant factor causing such illnesses as depression, anxiety, autism, and even schizophrenia. (Zhu, 2019; Shi, 2021; Góralczyk-Bińkowska, 2022). At the very least, if you have a happy, healthy gut, it will be easier to regulate your emotions and speak effectively.

Efforts to improve the balance of microbes in the gut have been tried by various means besides the common-sense dietary approach. Probiotic supplements in various mixtures, some with prebiotics, may be helpful. (Góralczyk-Bińkowska, 2022). Knocking out a specific strain of harmful bacteria with a well-designed, targeted antibiotic is helpful in some cases. (Mayer, 2022). However, we must watch out for "friendly fire" as the antibiotic might also kill helpful bacteria.

## Fecal Transplant

A more dramatic way to restore a healthy microbiome to a diseased gut is to transplant a mix of microbes from the gut of a healthy donor to the large bowel of a patient! (Socala, 2021; Zhu, 2019). Yes, researchers actually perform this! Imagine explaining that to your children or grandchildren!

Still, transplanting a slurry of feces from a healthy donor into the proximal large bowel of a diseased patient via colonoscope has proven to be effective. The earliest successful use of this was in treating Clostridium difficile (C. diff) infection. Research is actively proceeding to see if supplements or these fecal transplants will also successfully treat a wide range of psychiatric and neurodegenerative diseases.

# Wrapping Up

Our understanding of the gut-brain-throat axis will grow over the coming years, but for now, at least we know some ways to improve the function of that axis. In truth, it is vain to think we are discovering something entirely new. 2400 years ago, Hippocrates said, "Let food be your medicine." Doubtless, he got that idea from his mother.

Moms everywhere have surely been saying, "Eat your veggies!" for 10,000 years. It is impressive that, in most cases, after 100 years of research, having spent millions of hours and dollars in the lab discovering truly fascinating details, the moms of the world had it right eons ago—just eat your veggies and obey your mama!

It turns out that a diet consisting of high variety of vegetables promotes a healthy mix of bacteria in our gut. In general, these veggies, and many spices, have anti-inflammatory effects in the gut, and they provide food for the friendly bacteria that live there. Moms of the distant past also knew how to store one or two foods that can safely ferment—yogurt, buttermilk, sauerkraut, aged cheese, miso, chamoy sauce, and kimchi.

Observe how you feel an hour or so after eating one of these fermented foods and then how you feel for the next day or two. If you and your gut agree you feel good, include that in your diet. Again, it would make sense to have at least two such fermented foods frequently incorporated into your diet to cultivate a healthy gut microbiome.

Insofar as possible, use whatever healthy means available to prevent or mitigate excessive stress. Choose your foods and beverages wisely. Get enough sleep. Perform the amount of exercise that best suits you. Oh, and remember to laugh now and then! It's good for your physical and mental well-being!

# References:

Bonaz, B., Bazin, T., & Pellissier, S. (2018). The Vagus Nerve at the Interface of the Microbiota-Gut-Brain Axis. *Frontiers in Neuroscience*, *12*(49). https://doi.org/10.3389/fnins.2018.00049

Breit, S., Kupferberg, A., Rogler, G., & Hasler, G. (2018). Vagus Nerve as Modulator of the Brain–Gut Axis in Psychiatric and Inflammatory Disorders. *Frontiers in Psychiatry*, *9*(44). https://doi.org/10.3389/fpsyt.2018.00044

Chakrabarti, A., Geurts, L., Hoyles, L., Iozzo, P., Kraneveld, A. D., La Fata, G., Miani, M., Patterson, E., Pot, B., Shortt, C., & Vauzour, D. (2022). The microbiota–gut–brain axis: pathways to better brain health. Perspectives on what we know, what we need to investigate and how to put knowledge into practice. Cellular and Molecular Life Sciences, 79(2). https://doi.org/10.1007/s00018-021-04060-w

De Couck, M., Caers, R., Musch, L., Fliegauf, J., Giangreco, A., & Gidron, Y. (2019). How breathing can help you make better decisions: Two studies on the effects of breathing patterns on heart rate variability and decision-making in business cases. International Journal of Psychophysiology, 139, 1–9. https://doi.org/10.1016/j.ijpsycho.2019.02.011

Diener, C., Dai, C. L., Wilmanski, T., Baloni, P., Smith, B., Rappaport, N., Hood, L., Magis, A. T., & Gibbons, S. M. (2022).

Genome–microbiome interplay provides insight into the determinants of the human blood metabolome. *Nature Metabolism*, *4*(11), 1560–1572. https://doi.org/10.1038/s42255-022-00670-1

Góralczyk-Bińkowska, A., Szmajda-Krygier, D., & Kozłowska, E. (2022). The Microbiota–Gut–Brain Axis in Psychiatric Disorders. International Journal of Molecular Sciences, 23(19), 11245. https://doi.org/10.3390/ijms231911245

Magnon, V., Dutheil, F., & Vallet, G. T. (2021). Benefits from one session of deep and slow breathing on vagal tone and anxiety in young and older adults. Scientific Reports, 11(1). https://doi.org/10.1038/s41598-021-98736-9

Mayer, E. A., Nance, K., & Chen, S. (2022). The Gut–Brain Axis. Annual Review of Medicine, 73(1), 439–453. https://doi.org/10.1146/annurev-med-042320-014032

Shi, L., Ju, P., Meng, X., Wang, Z., Yao, L., Zheng, M., Cheng, X., Li, J., Yu, T., Xia, Q., Yan, J., Zhu, C., & Zhang, X. (2023). Intricate role of intestinal microbe and metabolite in schizophrenia. BMC Psychiatry, 23(1). https://doi.org/10.1186/s12888-023-05329-z

Socała, K., Doboszewska, U., Szopa, A., Serefko, A., Włodarczyk, M., Zielińska, A., Poleszak, E., Fichna, J., & Wlaź, P. (2021). The role of microbiota-gut-brain axis in neuropsychiatric and neurological disorders. Pharmacological

Research, 172, 105840.
https://doi.org/10.1016/j.phrs.2021.105840


Van Treuren, W., & Dodd, D. (2017). Microbial Contribution to the Human Metabolome: Implications for Health and Disease. Annual Review of Pathology: Mechanisms of Disease, 15(1). https://doi.org/10.1146/annurev-pathol-020117-043559


Zhu, F., Guo, R., Wang, W., Ju, Y., Wang, Q., Ma, Q., Sun, Q., Fan, Y., Xie, Y., Yang, Z., Jie, Z., Zhao, B., Xiao, L., Yang, L., Zhang, T., Liu, B., Guo, L., He, X., Chen, Y., & Chen, C. (2019). Transplantation of microbiota from drug-free patients with schizophrenia causes schizophrenia-like abnormal behaviors and dysregulated kynurenine metabolism in mice. Molecular Psychiatry. https://doi.org/10.1038/s41380-019-0475-4

# STEP TWO

## HEAL YOURSELF

*Observe when and why you speak. Listen to what you say and how you say it. As you do this, you can learn much about yourself—your emotions, triggers, strengths, and weaknesses. Use this information to heal. Ask for help to heal when needed. The idea is that if you do this with curiosity and a willingness to learn, your speaking will gain authenticity and effectiveness.*

# CHAPTER 5

## Embracing the Shadows

**"Know thyself."** —ancient Greek proverb, circa 500 B.C.

To speak well, you have to know who you are. The ancient Greeks knew that, and Carl Jung, a Swiss psychiatrist, around 1912, honed this pearl of wisdom into a powerful tool of psychology called "Shadow Work."

Shadow work involves exploring hidden parts of your personality—the "shadow self." This shadow self-harbors your suppressed negative and positive thoughts, emotions, and impulses.

By engaging in shadow work, you will uncover these hidden traits, bringing them into the light of consciousness.

# The Origin of Shadow Work

Carl Jung, a pioneer in psychology, first conceptualized the idea of the "shadow." According to Jung, the shadow is a part of your unconscious mind consisting of repressed weaknesses, shortcomings, and instincts. Everyone has a shadow, and it's often composed of the parts of ourselves we deny or dislike. Jung believed acknowledging and understanding your shadow is crucial for personal growth and self-awareness.

# The Process of Introspection and Self-Discovery

To heal and grow, you must confront and acknowledge the hidden parts of yourself. It's a path that requires courage, honesty, and a willingness to face what you may have chosen to ignore or suppress. By doing this, you will likely become aware of some traits or weaknesses that may repulse you. But you will also discover suppressed talents and positive traits long forgotten or suppressed.

### Recognizing and Accepting Your Suppressed Self

At the core of shadow work is recognizing and accepting the suppressed traits, emotions, and desires you've either consciously or unconsciously pushed aside. Often, these traits have been deemed unacceptable or inappropriate based on societal norms, personal beliefs, or past experiences. For many, this can include feelings of anger, jealousy, or sadness, as well as positive traits like assertiveness or creativity that were discouraged during childhood or in another social context.

## The Challenge of Facing the Uncomfortable

This journey can surface a range of emotions, from fear and shame to sadness and guilt. It's a process that demands vulnerability and honesty with yourself. The challenge lies not only in uncovering hidden traits, but also in learning to integrate them into your conscious life in a healthy and constructive way.

## The Role of Reflection and Mindfulness

Reflection and mindfulness are vital in this process. Shadow work often involves techniques like journaling, meditation, and guided introspection to help you discover your unconscious mind. These practices allow for a safe space to explore and understand these hidden aspects. Through mindful reflection, you can see how your shadow influences your thoughts, feelings, and, most importantly, your speech and communication patterns.

## Moving Towards Acceptance and Integration

The ultimate goal of shadow work is not just to uncover the shadow but to accept and integrate it. This means acknowledging these suppressed elements are a valid part of who you are and learning to embrace them. By doing so, you can start to heal and become whole, leading to a more authentic and balanced self. This acceptance is important for mindful speaking, as it allows you to communicate more honestly and effectively, free from the unconscious influences that previously held sway over your words and actions.

## The Shadow's Impact on Speech

Your shadow influences your speech and communication. It holds the keys to many of your triggers—those automatic, often negative reactions you have in certain situations. For instance, if you find yourself reacting angrily or defensively during conversations without fully understanding why, it's likely your shadow self is at play. These reactions can hinder effective communication and prevent you from engaging in truly mindful speaking.

## Unveiling Hidden Triggers in Communication

One of the key reasons shadow work is crucial in the context of mindful speaking is its ability to uncover the hidden emotional triggers often rooted in your shadow, which can lead to reactive and uncontrolled responses in conversations. By engaging in shadow work, you become aware of these triggers, understand their origins, and learn how to manage them. This awareness prevents you from making knee-jerk reactions and helps you to maintain composure and thoughtfulness in your speech.

## Enhancing Authenticity and Self-Awareness

Shadow work also promotes a deeper level of self-awareness and authenticity in communication. By acknowledging and integrating the suppressed traits, you can speak more honestly and from a place of wholeness. This authenticity is key to building trust and genuine connections with others. When you communicate from a place of full self-awareness, your words carry more weight and sincerity.

## Facilitating Emotional Regulation

Another critical aspect of shadow work in relation to mindful speaking is emotional regulation. By confronting and understanding the emotions residing in your shadow, you gain better control over them. This control is essential in situations where your speech needs to be measured and deliberate, allowing you to express yourself clearly without being overwhelmed by unprocessed emotions.

## Preparing for Effective Listening

Lastly, shadow work is not just about how you speak but also how you listen. Recognizing your own shadows can make you a more empathetic and understanding listener. It's like you acknowledge the beauty in you that arose from some past injury or irritation, such as the importance of empathy. And you can recognize that unique trait in others. You become more attuned to the underlying emotions and motivations in their speech. You listen better.

# Wrapping Up

In summary, the benefits of working with your unconscious mind to uncover parts of yourself that have been repressed and hidden from yourself, for whatever reason, cannot be overstated. Discussing shadow work in the context of mindful speaking is not just relevant but essential. It provides the tools for emotional regulation, self-awareness, and authenticity, all of which are contributing factors for controlling your tongue and engaging in meaningful, mindful communication.

In the next chapter, you will learn how to perform shadow work. We'll look at techniques and exercises that can help you integrate the insights gained from shadow work into your daily communication, leading to more effective, mindful, and empathetic interactions.

# CHAPTER 6

## Harnessing Shadow Work

**"A shadow cannot ignore the sun that all day creates and moves it."** —Rumi

To recap before we delve into techniques and exercises, the essence of shadow work is a transformative process introduced by Carl Jung as early as 1912 that involves confronting and integrating the hidden, often neglected parts of your personality. This journey is not just about self-awareness; it's about unlocking a more authentic and balanced way of expressing yourself.

By acknowledging both the positive and negative aspects that reside in your "shadow," you pave the way for more genuine and effective communication.

# Understanding Emotional Triggers: Unveiling the Hidden Catalysts

By engaging in shadow work, you unearth the deeper origins of what triggers you to speak in a way you later regret. These triggers are frequently rooted in repressed emotions or unresolved past experiences. Becoming aware of your triggers enables you to respond to situations with more thoughtfulness and less impulsivity, enhancing the quality and effectiveness of your communication.

## Common Emotional Triggers in Communication

**Criticism or Rejection:** Negative feedback or the feeling of being rejected can trigger defensive or aggressive responses, especially if linked to past events of inadequacy or rejection.

**Feeling Disrespected or Unheard:** Situations where you feel your opinions are disregarded or your dignity is undermined can trigger feelings of anger or frustration.

**Fear of Failure or Embarrassment:** The prospect of making mistakes or being embarrassed, often tied to past failures or humiliations, can lead to anxiety-driven responses.

**Loss of Control:** Situations where you feel powerless or out of control can trigger stress responses, often rooted in past experiences where you felt helpless.

**Personal Values Being Challenged:** When your core beliefs or values are questioned, it can trigger a strong emotional response, particularly if these values have been a source of conflict in the past.

**Unexpected Change or Uncertainty:** Humans naturally seek stability, so unexpected or uncertain situations can trigger anxiety, particularly if past changes have had adverse outcomes.

**Feeling Overwhelmed or Overburdened:** When you feel excessively pressured or overwhelmed, it can trigger stress responses, often linked to past experiences of being unable to cope.

By identifying these triggers and understanding their roots in your shadow, you can respond to them in more mindful and controlled ways. This process not only improves your communication but also contributes to your overall emotional well-being and personal growth.

# Positive Aspects in the Shadow: Rediscovering Hidden Strengths

Shadow work not only involves addressing and managing the negative aspects of our personality; it's also pivotal in uncovering and expressing the positive traits you may have suppressed. Various factors, such as societal norms, past traumas, or personal insecurities, can lead you to hide or downplay positive aspects of your personality. Shadow work allows you to rediscover these traits and integrate them into your way of communicating, enriching your interactions and making them more genuine and reflective of your true self.

## Key Positive Traits Uncovered Through Shadow Work

**Assertiveness:** Do you find yourself suppressing your assertive side to avoid conflict? Or have you suppressed your assertiveness through fear of being perceived as aggressive? If this is you, shadow work can help you reclaim this trait, enabling you to express your needs and opinions confidently and respectfully.

**Creativity:** Do you have a creative trait stifled by fear of judgment or failure? If so, shadow work encourages you to embrace your creativity, allowing for more innovative and imaginative communication.

**Empathy:** Some suppress their empathetic nature to protect themselves from emotional pain or vulnerability. Rediscovering this trait can lead to more compassionate interactions.

**Adventurousness:** A sense of adventure or willingness to take risks can be dampened by past failures or fears. Shadow work helps you recognize the value of exploring new ideas and perspectives in conversations.

**Joyfulness:** The ability to express joy and positivity can be overshadowed by past experiences of loss or disappointment. Reintegrating this trait can bring a more uplifting and positive tone to your interactions.

**Resilience:** Life's challenges can sometimes lead to downplaying your resilience. Rediscovering this trait helps you communicate with a sense of strength and perseverance, especially in difficult situations.

## Societal Expectations and Personal Suppression

One reason these positive traits end up in the shadow is societal expectations. Cultural norms and societal pressures can dictate what is acceptable or valued, leading you to suppress parts of yourself that don't align with these expectations. For instance, a person might hide their creative talents because they've been told it's not a practical career path, or they might suppress their assertiveness for a job role that imposes obedience and conformity.

## Personal Insecurities and Past Experiences

Personal insecurities and past experiences also play a significant role in pushing positive traits into the shadow. For example, if someone has ridiculed or criticized you for a particular trait or interest in the past, you might have chosen to suppress it to avoid further pain or rejection. This suppression is a defense mechanism, but it also means these positive qualities remain undeveloped and therefore do not enrich your life.

## The Role of Shadow Work in Unveiling Positive Traits

Shadow work can be a powerful tool in bringing these suppressed positive traits to light. By engaging in introspective practices, you learn to recognize and appreciate these hidden aspects of yourself. This process involves challenging your old beliefs and narratives keeping these traits buried and exploring new ways to integrate them into your identity and life.

## Enhancing Communication Through Rediscovered Traits

Uncovering and embracing these positive aspects can have a profound impact on how you communicate. For instance, rediscovering your assertiveness can lead to more confident and clearer communication. Embracing your creativity can add richness and depth to conversations. By integrating these positive traits, you not only enrich your own life but also enhance your interactions with others, leading to more authentic and effective communication.

## The Shadow's Gift of Positive Traits

In conclusion, the shadow is not just a repository of our fears and flaws; it's also a treasure trove of suppressed strengths and qualities. Through shadow work, you can rediscover these positive aspects and bring them to light, allowing them to enhance your ability to communicate and connect with others. This process is an integral part of personal growth and plays a crucial role in the art of mindful speaking.

# Engaging in Practical Exercises: Tools for Integrating Shadow Work into Mindful Speaking

To effectively integrate insights gained from shadow work into our daily communication, engaging in practical exercises can be most beneficial. Designed to foster self-awareness and reflection, exercises help us to understand and modify our speech patterns for more mindful and effective communication.

## Reflective Writing Prompt: Unraveling the Layers of Our Responses

**Purpose:** Reflective writing aims to dissect and understand your reactions in conversations, particularly those that didn't go as intended. By reflecting on these moments, you can uncover the hidden aspects of your shadow that may have influenced your responses.

**Process:** Think of a recent conversation where you reacted in a regrettable or unideal way. Record the specific trigger in the conversation—what was said or done that sparked your reaction. Detail your immediate response and then explore how you would have preferred to respond in that situation. Keep a notebook for this. Because it integrates different areas of the brain, I favor handwritten notes, but you may type it or use voice recorder.

**Exploration:** Look deeply into the aspects of your shadow that might have played a part in this interaction. Was there a suppressed emotion or trait that surfaced unexpectedly? How did this hidden aspect of your personality influence your reaction? Reflect on how acknowledging and understanding these shadow elements could lead to more controlled and thoughtful responses in future conversations.

## Two-Week Speech Diary: A Journey of Self— Discovery Through Daily Reflection

**Objective:** The goal of diary keeping is to develop a deeper understanding of your communication patterns. Write about your effective and ineffective speaking. By tracking daily speech, you can identify the emotional triggers and suppressed aspects of your personality that influence how you communicate.

**Method:** Maintain a diary for two weeks, focusing specifically on instances of your speech each day. In the evening, take time to reflect and note down moments where your communication was particularly effective or where it fell short of your expectations.

**Analysis:** With each entry, examine the underlying factors that shaped your speech. Consider how your emotions, past experiences, or aspects of your personality you usually suppress influenced how you communicated. Were there patterns in your responses linked to specific emotional triggers or suppressed traits?

**Outcome:** The aim of this exercise is not just to observe but to actively cultivate self-awareness and mindfulness in communication. By understanding the influences behind your speech, you can work towards modifying your responses, leading to more mindful, effective, and authentic interactions.

## The Impact of Self-Esteem on Communication

Self-esteem is a major factor in how you communicate. Recognizing your own value makes the pursuit of personal growth, including the refinement of your speech, a meaningful endeavor. High self-esteem allows you to approach shadow work and other self-improvement practices with a constructive and optimistic mindset. Adverse childhood experiences can make this challenging. So can things like mental illness or traumatic events. So, receive help from your physician or counselor if needed. We all need help now and then. No one can live their whole life without the help of another. And each of us is deserving of love and respect.

## Celebrating Communication Milestones

As you engage in shadow work and notice improvements in your communication, it's important to acknowledge and celebrate your progress! Recognizing and rewarding small victories and positive changes not only reinforces the value of this introspective work but also motivates you to continue on this path of growth.

## Wrapping Up

In summary, shadow work is an essential tool for enhancing your communication skills. By uncovering and integrating the suppressed aspects of your personality, you achieve a more authentic and effective way of speaking and listening. Engaging in reflective writing or two-week diaries, or both, helps you create a visual picture that may unveil patterns in your interactions, such as wanting to express a strong opinion about the world but holding back through fear of judgment, or correcting people who make spoken mistakes because you just can't let it go despite its negative impact. This journey towards mindful speaking is ongoing, and the insights gained from shadow work can lead to profound improvements in how you express yourself and connect with others.

It's now time to understand the power of pause, and the neuroscience behind it. The next chapter offers practical exercises to learn and incorporate in your quest to master the art of speech.

# CHAPTER 7

## Mastering the Art of the Pause in Speech

**"When angry, count to ten before you speak. If very angry, count to one hundred."** —Thomas Jefferson

In your journey of mindful speaking, mastering the art of pausing before you speak is critical. This chapter looks at the neuroscience behind pause, particularly the role of the prefrontal cortex, and offers practical exercises to develop this ability.

## The Neuroscience Behind Pausing

The neuroscience behind pausing in speech involves complex interactions between various brain regions and neural processes. Speech production itself is a highly coordinated process that relies on the integration of motor, sensory, and cognitive functions. The ability to pause just before speaking involves pathways in the brain that may vary somewhat across individuals, but there are commonalities. Fortunately, for those who wish to, these pathways can be modified, and new habits can be formed, including the habit of using a timely pause.

## Speech Regulation

While the prefrontal cortex is a key player in speech regulation, other parts of the brain also contribute significantly to this process. The brain's intricate network coordinates not only the production of speech but also the timing and appropriateness of your verbal responses. This involves a complex interplay between various brain regions, each contributing to the nuanced task of speech regulation.

## The Interplay of Cognitive and Emotional Processes

The ability to pause before speaking is not just a cognitive function; it also involves emotional processing. The limbic system, which deals with emotions, works in tandem with cognitive areas to influence your speech. When you pause, you're allowing time for both cognitive and emotional processing, ensuring your responses are not only well-thought-out but also emotionally appropriate. This balance is crucial in maintaining effective and empathetic communication.

## The Role of Memory and Experience

Your past experiences and memories, stored in different parts of the brain, sway how you formulate your responses. When you pause, you give yourself the opportunity to access these memories and experiences, allowing time for input from past learning and insight. This can be particularly useful in complex or challenging conversations where drawing upon previous experiences can guide your responses. It can even allow that moment it takes to recall an example of how a mentor would handle themselves in a similar situation.

## The Impact of Pausing on Neural Pathways

When you practice pausing before speaking, you strengthen neural pathways in your brain that will help you in the future. This reinforcement can lead to improved impulse control and better decision-making over time. As these neural pathways become more robust, pausing and reflecting before speaking becomes your new, habitual response, enhancing your overall communication skills. It becomes a part of who you are. Healthy self-esteem remains important, since most of us will make a few mistakes before this new habit is solid under duress. Be kind to yourself. And be thankful when you are mindful of these things and are making progress.

## The Brain's Adaptability and Learning

The brain's plasticity means it has the ability to adapt and learn new patterns of behavior. By consistently practicing the pause in your speech, you can train your brain to default to this technique. Adaptability is a powerful aspect of the brain that you can harness to improve not only your communication skills but also your overall cognitive function.

## Beyond the Prefrontal Cortex: A Holistic View

Understanding the neuroscience behind pausing before speaking requires a holistic view of the brain's functioning. It's not just about one area controlling your speech but a coordinated effort involving various parts of the brain. This complex orchestration ensures your speech is not only timely and appropriate but also reflective of your values, self-image, thoughts, emotions, creativity, and experiences.

# The Power of the Pause in Communication

Pausing before you speak is a simple yet powerful tool in effective communication. This brief moment of silence gives you the opportunity to engage your cognitive processes, collect your thoughts, consider the impact of your words, and choose how to articulate your message most effectively. This thoughtful reflection ensures your communication is not only clear but also considerate and aligned with your intentions.

## Enhancing Clarity and Precision in Speech

A pause allows you to sift through your thoughts and select the most appropriate words and tone for the situation at hand. This careful selection process leads to greater precision in your speech, helping you to convey your message more accurately.

By taking this moment to compose your thoughts, you can avoid ambiguities and misunderstandings that often arise from hasty or impulsive speech. The clarity gained through pausing can significantly enhance the quality of your interactions.

## Preventing Impulsive Reactions and Misunderstandings

One key benefit of pausing before speaking is the prevention of knee-jerk reactions that can lead to conflict or hurt feelings. In the heat of the moment, your emotions can drive you to say things you might later regret. We've all been there. By pausing, you give yourself the chance to cool down, assess the situation more objectively, and respond in a more thoughtful and less reactive way. This can be particularly valuable in emotionally charged or sensitive conversations, where impulsive words can escalate tensions or cause unnecessary harm.

## Creating Space for Meaningful Dialogue

Pausing not only benefits the speaker but also enriches the overall conversational experience. A well-timed pause can create a space for contemplation, allowing both the speaker and the listener to process the information being shared. This space can lead to deeper understanding and more meaningful exchanges, as it encourages active listening and thoughtful responses. In a world where conversations often feel rushed or superficial, the power of the pause can transform our interactions into more engaging and profound dialogues.

# Practical Exercises for Mastering the Pause

Believe it or not, there are practical exercises that can help you develop your ability to pause in a timely and purposeful manner.

## Meditation for Mindful Speaking

Meditation can be a powerful tool for developing the habit of pausing. Simple mindfulness exercises, such as focusing on your breath or observing your thoughts without judgment, can enhance your ability to pause before responding in conversations.

## Physical Activities that Encourage Pausing

Activities like swimming and yoga require a conscious awareness of breathing. This awareness can translate into a greater control over when and how you speak, teaching you to use pauses effectively.

## The Modified Speaking Fast

Try a 24- or 48-hour modified speaking fast. During this period, limit your speech to only essential communication. This exercise can heighten your awareness of your usual speaking patterns and the power of deliberate silence. Just be careful not to ignore anyone! I found a speaking fast to be one of the most effective ways to improve the mindfulness of my speaking. And through considerable trial and error, including some embarrassing slip-ups, I have found that in my case, at least, it's best if I repeat this fast once a month.

## Dramatic Arts and the Art of Pause

Engaging in drama or acting can be an excellent way to learn the strategic use of pause. Try participating in local theater or simple role-playing exercises to understand how pauses can add depth and meaning to speech.

## Singing: Harnessing the Power of Musical Pauses

Singing, much like acting, teaches the importance of timing and pause. Incorporating singing into your daily routine can help you become more conscious of the rhythm and flow of your speech. It doesn't matter if you have the singing voice of a strangled cat.

## Symbolic Reminders: The Pearl Analogy

Consider using pearls as a symbolic reminder to pause. Let it remind you that, with time, an irritation can be transformed into something beautiful and valuable  Wearing a pearl accessory can serve as a physical cue, reminding you to take a moment before speaking. This small gesture can have a significant impact on your communication habits. An alternative to wearing a pearl is to put up a poster or copy of Vermeer's "Girl with a Pearl Earring" where you work or live. There are also a variety of serious and humorous renditions of Vermeer's famous painting to choose from.

# Wrapping Up

Pausing is a key component in the art of mindful speaking. It allows you to communicate with greater intention, empathy, and impact. By learning to pause before speaking, you improve not only the effectiveness of your communication but also the quality of your relationships and interactions. This simple yet profound practice is essential for anyone looking to enhance their communication skills and engage in more meaningful conversations.

Mastering the art of the pause is a journey of self-awareness and practice. By engaging in exercises, whether it's singing, acting, swimming, meditation, or whatever tickles your fancy, you can develop a more controlled, thoughtful, and impactful way of speaking.

The next chapter will build upon these skills, showing how they contribute to more effective and mindful communication.

# CHAPTER 8

## Embrace Tone and Cadence

**"The tongue can paint what the eyes cannot see."**
—ancient proverb

Great orators, actors, and singers know this. Their career depends upon it. In fact, the impact of your words often lies not in your content but in delivery. This chapter focuses on the subtle yet powerful elements of tone and cadence, pivotal in shaping how your words are received and understood.

Tone and cadence are the unsung heroes of communication. They color your words, giving them emotion and rhythm. When you speak, it's not just a stream of words; it's a melody composed of varied pitches and pauses. By mastering these elements, you can transform your speech from an exchange of information into an engaging, memorable experience.

By embracing tone and cadence, you learn to express yourself more effectively. The right tone can convey empathy, authority, or enthusiasm, while the right cadence can make your speech more compelling and easier to follow. This chapter will guide you through understanding and harnessing these powerful tools in everyday communication.

## The Importance of Tone in Communication

Tone dictates how your messages are received. It's the emotional quality of your voice that accompanies the spoken words. Think of tone as the way your voice "sounds"—it can be happy, angry, sad, or excited. This aspect of communication is powerful because it often speaks louder than the actual words.

For instance, saying, "I'm fine" in a cheerful tone can convey genuine contentment, but the same words spoken in a flat, muted tone might suggest otherwise. In mindful speaking, being aware of your tone is essential. It's not just the words you choose, but the way you express them that impacts your listener. A mindful speaker pays attention to their tone, ensuring it aligns with their message and intention.

Understanding and controlling your tone can make a big difference in your interactions. A calm, steady tone can defuse tension, while an enthusiastic one can inspire and motivate those around you. By being conscious of your tone, you can enhance your ability to communicate effectively and connect with others.

## Cadence: The Rhythm of Speech

Cadence in speech is like the tempo in music. It's about how fast or slow you talk, and the rhythm you use when you're speaking. Just like a good song has a rhythm that keeps you hooked, your speech has a cadence that can either draw in your listeners or push them away.

A well-paced cadence is key to holding your audience's attention. If you speak too fast, your listeners might struggle to keep up. Too slow, and they might lose interest. It's about finding a balance. A varied cadence, with changes in speed and pauses, can make your speech more dynamic and interesting.

Think of cadence as the way you use the pace of your speech to emphasize your points. When you slow down, you signal that something important is coming. When you speed up, you convey excitement or urgency. By mastering cadence, you can make your speech not just easier to follow, but more engaging and effective.

## Integrating Pauses with Tone and Cadence

Combining pauses with tone and cadence is like adding

punctuation in writing. Just as commas and periods help to structure sentences on a page, pauses help to structure our speech when we talk. They give our listeners time to digest what we've said and anticipate what's coming next.

When you pause, you give your words more impact. It's like highlighting a sentence in a book. You're telling your listener, "This is important; pay attention." Pauses also give you a moment to breathe and think about what you're going to say next, helping you maintain a steady, effective tone and rhythm.

Using pauses effectively with tone and cadence can make your speech more powerful and persuasive. It's not just about stopping for a second; it's about using that break to enhance the way your message is received. A well-timed pause, combined with the right tone and pace, can make your words more memorable and impactful.

## Practical Exercises for Mastering Tone and Cadence

Having explored the significance of tone and cadence in effective communication, it's now time to put theory into practice. The following exercises are designed to enhance your awareness and control over these crucial aspects of speech. Ten different exercises are presented. Though you would likely benefit from practicing each of them, choose two or three that suit you. Then practice them regularly. By engaging in your chosen activities, you'll not only develop a deeper understanding of how tone and cadence influence your message, but also gain practical skills to apply in your everyday conversations.

These exercises range from simple self-reflection to interactive practices, each aimed at refining your ability to speak with intention and impact during your mindful speaking journey. Whether addressing a large audience or having a one-on-one conversation, mastering tone and cadence can transform the way you communicate.

**Poetry and Song Lyrics:** Choose a poem or song that resonates with you. First, read it aloud at your normal pace. Then, read it again, but slow down significantly, emphasizing different words and phrases. Notice how the tone and rhythm of your voice change the emotional impact of the words.

**The Ecclesiastes Exercise:** Solomon, the son of David, King of Israel, wrote many wise words, including the passage quoted below, about time. I have long appreciated this passage, so much so I committed it to memory. While doing so, I noticed when spoken aloud with optimal cadence, it takes precisely one minute to recite. Did Solomon intend for a passage about time to take exactly one minute to read aloud? I don't know. But it does make for an inspiring tone and cadence exercise.

Read aloud these ancient words from Solomon as they appear in the book of Ecclesiastes 3:1-8. Though you may use any version you like, I have quoted it below from the World English Bible version. Aim to read it out loud in exactly one minute. This exercise will help you get a feel for the natural rhythm and flow of speech. Pay attention to how pacing affects the delivery of the message.

*"For everything there is a season,*
*and a time for every purpose under heaven:*
*a time to be born,*
*and a time to die;*
*a time to plant,*
*and a time to pluck up that which is planted;*
*a time to kill,*
*and a time to heal;*
*a time to break down,*
*and a time to build up;*
*a time to weep,*
*and a time to laugh;*
*a time to mourn,*
*and a time to dance;*
*a time to cast away stones,*
*and a time to gather stones together;*
*a time to embrace,*
*and a time to refrain from embracing;*
*a time to seek,*
*and a time to lose;*
*a time to keep,*
*and a time to cast away;*

*a time to tear,*
*and a time to sew;*
*a time to keep silence,*
*and a time to speak;*
*a time to love,*
*and a time to hate;*
*a time for war,*
*and a time for peace."*
—*Ecclesiastes 3:1-8, World English Bible*

**Daily Conversation Analysis:** Throughout your day, consciously slow down your speech during conversations. After each interaction, reflect on how this change in pace affected the way your message was received and how it influenced the overall conversation. Include your observations in your shadow work journal.

**Record and Review:** Use a recording device to capture your speech in different scenarios—a formal presentation, a casual chat, or a debate. Listen to the recordings and note how your tone and cadence vary. This exercise helps in self-awareness and adjusting your speaking style to different contexts.

**Mirror Practice:** Stand in front of a mirror and talk about a subject you are passionate about. Observe your facial expressions and listen to the changes in your tone and cadence. Adjust your speech to better convey your message, using your expressions and voice as tools.

EMBRACE TONE AND CADENCE

**Handling Interruptions:** Have a conversation with someone who will intentionally interrupt you at random intervals. Practice maintaining a calm and steady tone and cadence, even when your train of thought is disrupted. This helps in building resilience and control in your speech.

**Reading Aloud with Emphasis:** Select a short piece of text and read it aloud multiple times, each time placing emphasis on different words. Notice how the change in emphasis alters the tone, meaning, and impact of the sentence.

**Silent Movie Narration:** Watch a scene from a silent film and narrate the actions and emotions of the characters. Experiment by varying your tone and pace to match the mood of the scene. This exercise helps in understanding how tone and cadence can convey emotion without words.

**Role-Playing:** Engage in role-playing activities where you adopt different characters, each with a unique speaking style. Focus on how changing your tone and cadence can effectively convey different personalities and emotions.

**Feedback Loop:** Converse with a friend or family member and ask them to provide immediate feedback on your tone and cadence. Use this feedback to make real-time adjustments to your speech. This exercise is valuable for understanding how others perceive your speaking style and making improvements.

By practicing these exercises, you'll gain a deeper understanding and control of your tone and cadence, enhancing your ability to communicate mindfully and effectively.

## Reminders for Effective Practice

As you embark on these practical exercises to enhance your tone and cadence, it's important to approach them with the right mindset and strategy. Here are some key reminders to help you practice effectively and make the most of your learning journey.

**Consistency is Key:** Regular practice is essential. Try to incorporate these exercises into your daily routine for better results.

**Mindful Awareness:** Be aware of your tone and cadence during the exercises. Mindfulness will help you notice subtle nuances and make necessary adjustments.

**Record and Review:** If possible, record your practice sessions. Listening to your recordings can provide insights into areas that need improvement.

**Seek Feedback:** Don't hesitate to ask for feedback from trusted friends or family members. External perspectives can be invaluable.

**Patience and Persistence:** Developing control over your tone and cadence takes time. Be patient with yourself and persist even if progress seems slow.

**Comfortable Environment:** Practice in a quiet and comfortable setting where you can focus without interruptions.

**Reflect on Progress:** Regularly reflect on your progress. Acknowledge the improvements, no matter how small, and identify areas for further development.

**Stay Relaxed:** Ensure you are physically relaxed before starting the exercises. Tension in your body can affect your voice.

**Embrace Mistakes:** Mistakes are part of the learning process. Embrace them as opportunities to learn and grow.

**Enjoy the Process:** Remember, the goal is not just to improve but also to enjoy mastering the art of mindful speaking.

These reminders are designed to guide and support you through the exercises, helping you to practice effectively and enjoy the learning process.

## Personal Reflection and Application

In my own experience, speaking too rapidly was a common

challenge, especially in public settings. Nervousness often took the driver's seat, leading to hurried speech that sometimes muddled my message. However, with conscious effort and practice, I began to appreciate the power of controlling my tone and cadence.

This transformation was gradual but profound. I started to slow down, paying attention to how I articulated each word and phrase. This deliberate approach allowed me to convey my thoughts more clearly and confidently. The change in my speaking style also changed my experience of speaking. I began to enjoy the process, feeling more connected to my words and my audience.

The most rewarding part was noticing the audience's reaction. When I spoke with a controlled tone and measured cadence, people listened more attentively. Their engagement was visible—nods, smiles, and thoughtful expressions. This feedback was not just affirming; it was motivating. It reinforced the value of the skills I was developing.

This personal journey taught me that mastering tone and cadence isn't just about effective communication; it's about enjoying the art of speaking. It's about the satisfaction that comes from knowing your words are not just heard but felt and understood. This realization has been a cornerstone in my approach to mindful speaking.

# Dealing with Interruptions

Dealing with interruptions during a conversation can be challenging. It's easy to get flustered or annoyed, but the key is to stay calm and composed.

Here's how you can handle interruptions effectively:

**Stay Calm:** When someone interrupts you, take a deep breath. This simple act can help you maintain your composure and prevent a reactive response.

**Use a Steady Tone:** Responding in a calm and steady tone can help de-escalate the situation. It shows that you're in control of your emotions and are not easily rattled by interruptions or distractions.

**Keep Your Cadence Deliberate:** Instead of speeding up your speech in response to an interruption, maintain a deliberate pace. This helps in keeping your thoughts organized and ensures your message remains clear.

**Pause Before Responding:** If you're interrupted, pause for a moment before you continue. This pause gives you time to collect your thoughts and signals to the interrupter that you were not finished speaking. It also gives you a moment to regain your train of thought.

**Politely Assert Yourself:** If the interruptions persist, it's okay to politely assert yourself. You might say, "I understand your point, but I'd like to finish my thought."

**Refocus the Conversation:** After an interruption, gently steer the conversation back to your original point. This helps keep the discussion on track.

**Have an exit strategy. And remember, there might be a medical illness causing pressure of speech:** The physicians and mental health workers out there know this all too well. If someone is having a hyperthyroid storm or is in the acute manic phase of bipolar disorder or any number of other ailments, they might not be able to slow or pause their speech.

Sometimes, it's best to say, "I have to step out for a moment, but I'll be back" or "I will get someone in here who can help you." Then leave and get some help.

Remember, the way you handle interruptions can significantly impact the effectiveness of your communication. By staying calm and removing yourself from an awkward situation, or using a steady tone and deliberate cadence, you can navigate these situations with grace and maintain control of the conversation. At least you can control yourself in the conversation.

# Wrapping Up: Mastering Tone and Rhythm in Speech

Mastering tone and cadence is a key aspect of effective communication and speaking mindfully. It's about more than just choosing the right words; it's about how those words are delivered, and how they resonate with your target audience. This chapter has highlighted the importance of tone – the emotional quality of your voice – and cadence – the rhythm and pace of your speech. Together, they play a lead role in how your message is received.

As you embark on this journey of refining your tone and cadence, remember it's a process of self-discovery. You're not just learning a skill; you're exploring different facets of your personality and how they manifest in your speech. This exploration can be enlightening and deeply rewarding.

# STEP THREE

## MASTER YOURSELF

*Learn how to make the practice of mindful speaking fun and effective. Enjoy the process! Make it a part of your daily routine until it becomes automatic and a part of who you are.*

# CHAPTER 9

## Visualize and Simulate Success

**"Imagine with all your mind, believe with all your heart, achieve with all your might."** —origin unknown.

This quote highlights the power of visualization and simulation, not just for athletes, astronauts, or aspiring politicians, but for anyone, including those improving communication skills. Imagine a professional visualizing a confident speech or a parent mentally preparing for a conversation with their child. These techniques can shift your communication approach from nervousness to confidence, from confusion to clarity.

Visualization and simulation are conducive to mastering your speech. By mentally rehearsing successful interactions, you prepare your mind and body for effective, thoughtful, real-life conversations. It's not just about imagining success; it's about actively training your mind for it throughout your daily communications.

## The Science of Visualization

Visualization is a practical, science-backed process, not mere fantasy. When you visualize, you're doing more than just imagining a scenario; you're actively engaging your brain in a way that closely mimics real-life action. This is because the act of visualization stimulates the same neural pathways in your brain used when you actually perform the task.

For instance, when you visualize yourself speaking confidently in front of a large crowd, your brain is processing this scenario much like it would if you were actually doing it. This mental rehearsal helps in building and strengthening the neural connections associated with your speaking skills. You are running a simulation in your mind, preparing you for the actual event.

This technique is powerful. By visualizing yourself effectively, you're not just hoping for a positive outcome. You are wiring your brain to make it happen. It's a method of mental training that makes success a habit before you even face any given situation. It primes you for real-life interactions, ensuring when the moment comes, your brain is already familiar with what needs to be done.

VISUALIZE AND SIMULATE SUCCESS

# Case Studies of Success Through Visualization

**NASA's Moon Landing:** NASA's historic moon landing is a prime example of visualization effectiveness. Before the Apollo 11 astronauts ever left Earth, they spent countless hours visualizing and simulating every aspect of the mission. Through simulation, they practiced everything, from the lunar landing to walking on the moon's surface. This rigorous mental and physical rehearsal was key to their successful landing on the moon. It demonstrates how visualization can prepare you for complex tasks, ensuring you're ready for every scenario.

**The Romero Brothers:** The Romero Brothers, a renowned classical Spanish guitar group, have shown the world how visualization can start from a young age and shape a lifetime of success. Growing up in a musical family, they began visualizing themselves as performers early in their lives. This continuous mental rehearsal, coupled with physical practice, played a significant role in their development as musicians. Their journey illustrates how consistent visualization from childhood can lead to mastery in a chosen field.

**Eliud Kipchoge's Marathon Record:** Eliud Kipchoge's breaking of the two-hour barrier in the marathon is a powerful testament to the role of the mind in achieving physical feats. Before the race, Kipchoge spent countless hours visualizing his victory, going over the course, the pace, and the feeling of crossing the finish line in under two hours. This mental preparation was as rigorous and beneficial as his physical training. Kipchoge's achievement shows that visualization can be a key factor in surpassing limits and achieving what was once thought impossible. In so doing, he paved the way for the next generation of distance runners.

These stories show how powerful visualization can be. In each case, people used their imagination first to see themselves succeeding. They prove that whether you're an athlete, musician, scientist, or just trying to speak better, picturing success in your mind helps make it happen in real life.

## Visualizing Success in Everyday Conversations

In your daily life, you encounter situations where effective communication is key. Whether a meeting at work, a difficult conversation with a loved one, a public speaking event, or casual daily interactions, how you express yourself can significantly impact the outcome.

Visualization can be a powerful tool in preparing for these scenarios. By mentally rehearsing successful communication in various everyday situations, you can enhance your ability to handle these interactions with confidence and clarity.

Let's explore some common scenarios where visualization can make a meaningful difference.

## Scenario 1: The Workplace Meeting

Imagine you have an upcoming team meeting at work where you need to present an idea. Before the meeting, take a few minutes to visualize the scene. See yourself entering the room confidently, presenting your ideas clearly, and responding to questions with poise. Envision your colleagues' positive reactions and the feeling of accomplishment. This mental rehearsal can calm your nerves and prepare you to handle the actual situation more effectively.

## Scenario 2: A Difficult Conversation with a Loved One

Consider a situation where you need to have a challenging conversation with a family member or friend. Visualize the conversation in advance. Picture yourself listening actively, speaking calmly, and expressing your feelings without aggression. Imagine a resolution or at least a peaceful exchange of viewpoints. This visualization can help you approach the actual conversation with a more balanced and empathetic mindset and can defuse frustrations and anger.

## Scenario 3: Public Speaking

If you're preparing for a public speaking engagement, visualize the audience engaging with your speech, see yourself delivering your message with confidence and clarity, and hear the applause at the end. This practice can boost your confidence and reduce anxiety before the actual event.

### Scenario 4: Daily Interactions

Even for regular daily interactions, such as a conversation with a neighbor or a discussion with your child's teacher, picture these interactions going smoothly. Visualize yourself listening well, and speaking with content and delivery that adds value to those who listen. Picture yourself proceeding calmly and logically, even if you are confronted by someone speaking in a manipulative or aggressive manner.

### Scenario 5: Job Interview

Preparing for a job interview can be nerve-wracking. Visualize yourself walking into the interview room, greeting the interviewers with a confident smile, and sitting down calmly. Imagine yourself answering questions with clarity, showcasing your skills and experiences effectively, and leaving a positive impression. This mental rehearsal can help reduce anxiety and increase your confidence during the actual interview.

## Simulation: The Practice Ground

Simulation is a rehearsal for real-life communication, allowing you to practice in a safe, controlled environment. For example, before a sensitive talk with a colleague, simulate the conversation, anticipating various responses and practicing your reactions. This prepares you for different outcomes and builds confidence. Similarly, for public speaking, set up a mock environment and practice your speech, focusing on posture, gestures, eye contact, and voice modulation. This method helps refine your speaking skills, making you more prepared and confident for the actual event.

To effectively use simulation to improve your speaking skills, you can follow these 5 simplified steps:

1. **Choose Your Scenario:** Identify the specific situation you want to prepare for, such as a job interview, a difficult conversation with a friend, or a public speaking engagement.

2. **Set the Stage:** Create an environment that mimics the actual setting. If it's a meeting, arrange a similar setup; for public speaking, stand as if in front of an audience.

3. **Outline and Rehearse:** Write down key points or scripts and practice them. Focus on your tone, pace, and body language. If it's a conversation, consider possible responses and how you would handle them.

4. **Feedback and Adjustment:** Involve someone else to act as your audience or conversation partner. After

practicing, request feedback and adjust your approach based on what you learn.

5. **Repeat and Refine:** Continuously practice and refine your approach. The more you simulate, the more confident and prepared you'll become for the actual situation.

# The Role of Repetition in Habit Formation

To form new habits, consistent repetition is essential. It typically takes about 66 repetitions to establish a new habit, including improving speaking skills. To advance from habit formation to skill competence, about 300 repetitions are needed, where comfort and confidence in the skill grow. Mastery, however, may require approximately 10,000 repetitions, a process of gradual improvement. The quality of the practice will, of course, affect how many repetitions are needed at each level.

This principle of repetition is crucial for both visualization and simulation exercises in communication. Regular practice of these techniques, whether through mental rehearsal or simulated scenarios, ingrains these skills, making mindful speaking become more natural over time. Each repetition is a step closer towards integrating these skills into your daily behavior.

Here are some steps and tips to effectively incorporate repetition into your habit formation, particularly in the context of improving speaking skills through visualization and simulation:

**Establish a Consistent Practice:** Set aside a specific time each day for visualization and simulation exercises. Even a short daily session of 5-10 minutes can greatly impact your progress.

**Diversify Your Scenarios:** Practice a variety of scenarios to enhance your adaptability. For example, visualize different speaking situations, from casual conversations to formal presentations and confrontational ones, where de-escalation skills become relevant.

**Track and Reflect:** Keep a journal to monitor your repetitions and reflect on each practice session. Note what works well and any areas for improvement, helping you refine your approach.

**Seek Feedback and Adjust:** Whenever possible, get feedback on your practice from someone you trust. Use their insights to make adjustments and improve your technique.

**Apply Skills in Real Life:** Actively look for opportunities to apply what you've practiced in real-life situations. The more you use these skills in actual conversations, the quicker they will become a natural part of your communication style.

# Mnemonic for Mindful Speaking

When it comes to mindful speaking, having a quick and effective strategy to manage stressful situations is crucial. This is where the mnemonic "Oh Pearls" comes into play. It's a simple yet powerful tool designed to guide you through challenging moments, ensuring your responses are thoughtful, measured, and effective. By breaking down each component of this mnemonic, you learn to navigate difficult conversations with greater ease and composure. Create your own mnemonic, or use mine, inspired by how a pearl is formed from irritation:

**Oh – Take a Deep Breath:** Start by taking a deep breath. This helps to calm your mind and body, giving you a moment to collect your thoughts. It also stimulates your parasympathetic nervous system, slowing your heart rate and quieting that fight-or-flight response.

**Pause – Give Yourself a Moment:** After your deep breath, pause. This brief moment allows you to stop and think before you speak, preventing impulsive reactions. This allows your prefrontal cortex to get involved rather than allow a purely reflexive response.

**Evaluate – Consider Your Response:** Think about the situation and what response would be most appropriate. Consider the impact of your words before you say them.

**Action – Speak if Necessary:** If you decide it's appropriate to respond, do so calmly and clearly. Remember, sometimes the best action is to say nothing at all.

**Re-evaluate – Assess the Situation Again:** After you've spoken, take a moment to reflect on the situation again. Did your response help to resolve or improve the situation?

**Learn – What Can You Learn from This?:** Every interaction is a learning opportunity. Think about what worked well and what could be improved for next time.

**Safe Exit – Leave the Situation if Needed:** If the situation isn't improving or is becoming more stressful, it's okay to politely excuse yourself. Sometimes, the best option is to step away.

## Exercises for Mindful Speaking

This section introduces exercises for mindful speaking, focusing on the "Oh Pearls" mnemonic. Through daily reflection, role-playing, journaling, and positive affirmations, these exercises aim to embed mindful communication into your daily life. Regular practice will make "Oh Pearls" an instinctive part of your approach to challenging conversations.

**Daily Reflection:** At the end of each day, reflect on conversations where you felt agitated or stressed. Replay these moments in your mind and walk through the "Oh Pearls" steps. Ask yourself, how could you have applied each step in those situations?

**Role-Playing:** Practice in front of a mirror, or even better— practice with a friend or family member. Create scenarios where you might feel provoked or stressed. As you role-play these situations, consciously apply the "Oh Pearls" steps. Trust me, this exercise massively helps in preparing you for real-life situations.

**Journaling:** Keep a journal to note down instances where you successfully used "Oh Pearls." You could use the same notebook as for your shadow work. Write about the situation, how you applied each step, and the outcome. This will help you track your progress and understand the effectiveness of the mnemonic in different scenarios.

**Mindful Pauses:** Whenever you feel the onset of agitation, consciously pause and mentally go through the "Oh Pearls" steps. This practice helps in gradually replacing impulsive reactions with thoughtful responses.

**Positive Affirmations:** Alongside using "Oh Pearls," regularly practice positive affirmations related to mindful speaking. Affirmations like, "I speak with calm and clarity" or "I handle stressful conversations with ease" can reinforce your commitment to positive speech patterns. By regularly practicing these exercises, you'll find that using "Oh Pearls" becomes more instinctive, leading to more mindful and effective communication in your daily life.

# Integrating Visualization with Previous Chapters

To fully harness the power of visualization, it's important to integrate it with the techniques discussed in previous chapters. Here's how you can do it:

**Visualize Pausing:** Recall what we have discussed about the power of pausing. Now, visualize yourself in a conversation. Before responding, see yourself taking a deliberate pause. Feel how doing this slows your heart rate and relaxes you. This pause gives you time to think and respond more effectively. Imagine how this pause helps you control the flow of conversation.

**Tone Visualization:** Think back to what we have learned about tone. Visualize yourself speaking in different tones—calm, assertive, compassionate. See how your tone affects the listener's response. Seeing that successful response is rewarding, thereby reinforcing this new skill of yours. By visualizing the impact of your tone, you can better understand how to modulate it in real conversations.

**Cadence in Visualization:** Remember the lessons on cadence. In your mind, play out a scenario where you're speaking. Focus on the rhythm and pace of your speech. Visualize yourself speaking too quickly, then adjust to a more measured, effective cadence. Notice how this change in cadence makes your speech clearer and more engaging.

## Scenario: A Job Interview

Imagine you have an upcoming job interview for an exciting, new position. This scenario is perfect for integrating the visualization techniques from the previous chapters.

**Night Before the Interview - Visualization Session:**

- **Pausing:** Visualize yourself in the interview room. As the interviewer asks a question, see yourself taking a brief pause. This pause gives you a moment to collect your thoughts and respond carefully.

- **Tone:** Now, focus on how you're answering. Visualize yourself speaking with a confident yet friendly tone. Your tone conveys enthusiasm for the role and respect for the interviewer.

- **Cadence:** Pay attention to your pace of speech in this visualization. Adjust so it's clear and measured, ensuring your answers are well-articulated and easy to follow.

**Day of the Interview - Application:**

- **Pausing in Action:** During the actual interview, remember the visualization from the night before. When asked a question, consciously take that brief pause. This not only helps you answer more effectively but also shows that you're thoughtful and composed.

- **Tone in Reality:** Keep your tone in mind as you speak. Remember how you visualized your tone the night before and try to replicate that. A well-modulated tone can make a significant difference in how your responses are perceived.

- **Maintaining Cadence:** Be mindful of your speech's rhythm and pace. If you find yourself speaking too quickly due to nerves, slow down to the cadence you practiced in your visualization.

By applying these visualized techniques in a real-life scenario like a job interview, you significantly enhance your communication effectiveness. This integrated approach not only prepares you mentally but also boosts your confidence, knowing you've rehearsed these aspects in your mind.

# Wrapping Up: Harnessing the Power of Mindful Visualization

The journey to becoming a master communicator is significantly enhanced by the practice of visualization and simulation. These aren't just abstract concepts; they are practical, actionable tools that can lead to real improvements in the way you speak and interact. You are rewiring your brain for success.

**Regular Practice:** The key to harnessing these tools is regular, consistent practice. Just as athletes and musicians dedicate time to visualize their performances, you have to set aside moments in your daily routine to visualize successful communication scenarios.

**Transformative Impact:** Through visualization, you can mentally rehearse various speaking situations—from challenging conversations to public speaking events. This mental rehearsal primes your brain, making you more prepared and confident when the actual moment arrives.

**Enhancing Enjoyment:** Not only does this practice make your speech more effective, but it also makes the act of communicating more enjoyable. When you are less anxious and more prepared, you find joy in the art of conversation and public speaking.

**A Lifelong Skill:** Remember, mastering mindful speaking is a lifelong journey. Each visualization and simulation exercise is a step towards becoming a more articulate, confident, and effective communicator.

Visualization and simulation are not just tools for improvement; they are pathways to a richer, more fulfilling experience in the world of communication. By embracing these techniques, you open yourself up to a world where your words are not just heard but felt and remembered positively.

Having previously looked at how your speaking habits are formed from a neuroscience perspective, and now how you can advance from habit formation to skill competence in approximately 300 repetitions, it's time to go deeper into changing speech habits using behavioral modification techniques.

# CHAPTER 10

## Use Tools of Behavioral Modification

**"Words are, of course, the most powerful drug used by mankind."** —Rudyard Kipling, in a speech to the Royal College of Surgeons, London, 1923.

In communication, your speech is powerful and heavily influenced by habit. This chapter builds on what we've learned about the brain and speech habits. We'll explore practical ways to change how we speak using behavioral modification techniques. Whether it's reducing swearing or improving public speaking, these methods can help you communicate better.

# Revisiting Chapter 3: Unraveling the Science Behind Habit Transformation

In Chapter 3, we covered how your speaking habits are formed in the brain. We learned that the basal ganglia, located in the deep center of the brain, play a major role in forming habits. This is where your repetitive speaking patterns become automatic. We also discovered the habit loop: a cue triggers an action, leading to a reward. The reward increases the likelihood that you will repeat the activity. Awareness of this loop helps you understand why you speak the way you do.

We talked about how neurotransmitters like dopamine and serotonin are involved in forming and keeping habits. Dopamine helps reinforce behaviors that we find rewarding, while serotonin affects our mood and motivation.

Finally, we covered neuroplasticity, the brain's ability to change and form new connections. This is important because it means you can change your speaking habits with practice and effort.

# Practical Speaking Improvement Techniques

Now, in this chapter, we're going to use that knowledge to learn about behavioral modification techniques. These are practical methods you can use to change the way you speak. We'll look at two specific examples: stopping inappropriate swearing and becoming comfortable with public speaking. But you can apply these techniques to any speaking habit you desire to change.

We'll explore two main methods: Operant Conditioning and Acceptance and Commitment Therapy (ACT). Operant Conditioning uses rewards and consequences to change your habits. ACT focuses on being aware of your thoughts and behaviors without judging them. ACT can be thought of as an application of shadow work.

The aim of this chapter is to give you useful tools to change your speaking habits, all based on science. Let's get started!

## Setting Personal Goals

To effectively apply behavioral modification techniques, it's crucial to have clear and personal goals for your speaking habits. Identifying specific areas for improvement will guide you in using these methods more effectively.

### Understanding Personal Speaking Goals

Begin by pinpointing the aspects of your speech you wish to enhance. Whether decreasing your use of swear words, gaining confidence in public speaking, or dealing better with conflict, be specific about what you want to accomplish. For example, rather than a vague goal like, "I want to improve my speaking," a more precise aim would be, "I want to stop using swear words in professional settings." I plead guilty!

## Setting the Stage: Defining Your Communication Improvement Goals

**Stopping Inappropriate Swearing:** Identify when and where you're most likely to use swear words. Recall any lessons learned from doing shadow work. What triggers your swearing, and why? Knowing your triggers is the first step to addressing this habit.

**Enjoying Public Speaking:** Determine the specific challenges you face with public speaking. Is it anxiety, lack of preparation, or something else? Recognizing these hurdles allows you to focus on overcoming them.

**Enhancing Listening Skills:** Improving how you listen can dramatically affect your overall communication. Set a goal to become a better listener, which could involve practicing active listening techniques, like fully concentrating on the speaker, understanding their message, and responding thoughtfully.

Each of these goals serves as a starting point. You may have other areas in your speech you'd like to work on. The important thing is to be specific and understand why these goals are significant to you. This will help you effectively apply behavioral techniques for meaningful improvement.

# First Tool: Operant Conditioning

Operant Conditioning is a key technique for modifying behavior, including how we speak and communicate.

## Understanding the Basics of Operant Conditioning

Operant Conditioning hinges on a simple yet powerful concept: our behaviors are shaped by their consequences. When a behavior results in a positive outcome, we're naturally inclined to repeat it. Conversely, if the outcome is negative, we're less likely to engage in that behavior again. This principle is particularly relevant and effective when applied to modifying speaking habits.

In the context of speech, Operant Conditioning can be used to encourage desirable communication patterns and discourage unproductive ones. For instance, if your goal is to reduce the frequency of interrupting others during conversations, you might decide to implement a small penalty for each interruption, such as putting a dollar in a jar or doing five minutes of additional chores. This tangible consequence helps create awareness and gradually reduces unwanted behavior. It also helps to decrease the likelihood of the behavior recurring.

On the other hand, if you successfully engage in a challenging conversation with clarity and confidence, rewarding yourself reinforces this positive behavior, making it more likely that you'll approach future conversations in a similar manner. For example, after a successful conversation, you might buy another fun book to read, or indulge yourself in some leisurely window shopping just for fun. These types of rewards can provide a pleasant incentive to continue developing your communication skills.

This approach to behavior modification is not just about external rewards or punishments; it's about fostering a deeper awareness of how your actions lead to specific outcomes. By understanding and applying the principles of Operant Conditioning, you can actively work towards developing more effective and mindful speaking habits.

## Applying Operant Conditioning to Mindful Speaking Skills

**Setting Small, Attainable Goals:** Start with small, achievable goals in your speaking habits. For example, practice your response to aggravating situations in front of a mirror in your home twice per week. Role-play with your reflection what might trigger you to swear, then practice pausing, taking a deep breath, and responding in a positive manner. Or, if your goal is to improve your public speaking, practice in your living room in front of an imaginary audience once daily. Use a paper or smartphone calendar to remind you to practice.

**Rewarding Progress and Practice:** Recognize and reward your progress. This could be as simple as treating yourself to something enjoyable after a day of mindful speaking or a successful practice session. Consider making your own list of punishments and rewards ahead of time. Write it down and keep it somewhere accessible, like on your phone, or in your wallet or purse. This pre-planning helps you stay committed and makes rewarding or penalizing yourself more straightforward and consistent.

**Self-Monitoring:** Regularly track your speaking habits, noting both successes and areas for improvement. This helps to maintain awareness of your progress. A hand-written journal works well for this.

**Feedback from Others:** Get feedback on your speaking from people you trust. Their perspectives can provide valuable insights and motivation.

**Increasing Challenges:** As you improve, gradually raise your goals. For example, extend your public speaking time as you get more comfortable.

## Applying Operant Conditioning to Stop Inappropriate Swearing

**Daily Rewards for Journaling Successes and Slip-ups:** Keep a journal of your speaking habits. Reward yourself for journaling consistently. Further reward yourself for days when you successfully reduce swearing. These rewards could be anything that brings you joy, like binge-watching a drama series.

**Example of Punishment:** The "Swear Jar": Implement a consequence like adding money to a swear jar every time you cuss inappropriately. Then, after a specific period, collect the money and buy something valuable for the office, home, or whoever might have been offended by your profanity.

**Identify Triggers:** Recognize situations or emotions that prompt swearing. Awareness of these triggers can help you anticipate and control the urge to swear.

**Substitute Phrases:** Develop a list of alternative phrases or words to use instead of swear words. Practicing these substitutes can gradually replace the swearing habit. Even the phrase "Oh Pearls" or simply "Pearls" could be alternatives that would serve to remind you to take a deep breath, pause, evaluate, act if needed, learn from the experience, and safely remove yourself from a situation if that is the wisest move.

**Accountability Partner:** Communicate your objective to a friend or coworker who can keep you accountable. Regular check-ins with this person can strengthen your dedication to making a change.

## Applying Operant Conditioning to Enjoy Public Speaking

**Rewarding Practice Sessions:** It's important to give yourself a reward for each public speaking practice session you complete. Emphasize rewarding the effort you put into practice rather than just accomplishing your goals. This is especially important if your goal is highly competitive, like winning the UCLA Debate Invitational. Consistently rewarding your practice helps build a positive association with the effort itself, making it more likely you'll continue and improve over time.

**Consequences for Skipping Practice:** If you skip a practice session, set a small consequence like completing an extra chore.

**Visualization Techniques:** Before each practice session, spend a few minutes visualizing a successful speech. This can build confidence and reduce anxiety.

**Public Speaking Groups:** Join a group or club focused on public speaking. Participating in a supportive community can enhance your skills and enjoyment.

**Small Audience Practice:** Start by speaking in front of a small, familiar audience. Gradually increase the audience size as your comfort grows.

## Applying Operant Conditioning to Emphasize Positive Reinforcement

**Ratio of Praise to Correction:** Focus more on rewarding good behavior (positive reinforcement) than punishing bad behavior. A good ratio is about five rewards for every punishment.

**Intermittent Positive Reinforcement:** Randomly rewarding good behavior can be more effective than a predictable pattern. List several rewards, from a simple "Good job!" to a fun outing. Then, roll a dice to pick a random reward after each practice. This approach keeps your motivation fresh, exciting, and high, similar to how gambling can become addictive due to its unpredictable rewards. Except here, you always win. It's just a matter of how much you win on any particular occasion.

**Self-Compliments:** Acknowledge your own progress in speaking. Self-recognition acts as a motivator and builds confidence.

**Reward Variety:** Mix up the types of rewards you give yourself. This can range from small treats to leisure activities, keeping the reinforcement exciting.

**Progress Milestones:** Set specific milestones in your speaking improvement journey. Celebrate these achievements as a form of positive reinforcement.

## Utilizing Operant Conditioning for Better Communication

Through Operant Conditioning, you can effectively reshape your speaking habits into more thoughtful and impactful forms. This method provides a structured way to monitor and improve your communication. By consistently rewarding positive speaking behaviors and addressing negative ones, you'll enhance how you express yourself. This practice not only improves your interactions but also aids in your personal growth. In essence, Operant Conditioning guides you towards more effective and confident communication skills.

# Acceptance and Commitment Therapy (ACT)

Acceptance and Commitment Therapy (ACT) focuses on helping individuals live and behave consistently with their personal values while developing psychological flexibility. It emphasizes accepting what is out of your personal control and committing to action that improves and enriches your life.

## Connection with Shadow Therapy Principles

Like shadow work, ACT underscores the importance of being aware of and accepting thoughts and behaviors without judgment. Both therapies encourage embracing every part of oneself, including the less favorable aspects, and using this awareness for personal growth.

## Applying ACT to Stop Swearing Inappropriately

**Mindful Recognition:** Notice each time you swear. This awareness helps you understand your habit's frequency and context without self-judgment.

**Identifying Triggers:** Determine what prompts you to swear. Is it stress, anger, or a specific environment? Understanding triggers is key to changing this behavior.

**Value-based Alternatives:** Reflect on your core values and find alternative expressions that align with them, replacing swear words. Alternatively, if feasible, change your environment to avoid the triggers.

**Progress Tracking:** Keep a log of your swearing and any reductions. This helps recognize and reinforce your efforts.

**Emotional Acceptance:** Accept the emotions that lead to swearing, like frustration, without acting on them through swearing. This is central to ACT's approach.

## Applying ACT to Enjoy Public Speaking

**Accepting Anxiety:** First, understand feeling nervous about public speaking is normal. If your nerves feel overwhelming, consider using biofeedback, such as those that detect how much your hands sweat and transduce that to an audible pitch. With practice, you can decrease your anxiety response. Or talk to your doctor about a low-dose beta-blocker. This medication helps calm the effects of adrenaline and can be taken a couple of hours before you speak. You might only need it a few times before your mind becomes accustomed to speaking confidently without it. Remember, seeking help is a smart way to manage your anxiety and improve your public speaking.

**Focused Practice:** Regularly practice public speaking in a non-judgmental setting. This helps in building both comfort and skill.

**Value-based Speaking Goals:** Set speaking goals that align with your personal values, like sharing knowledge or connecting with others.

**Celebrating Small Wins:** Each successful speaking engagement, no matter how small, should be acknowledged as a step towards your goal.

**Mindful Reflection:** After public speaking, reflect on the experience positively, focusing on what you learned rather than how you performed.

## Applying ACT to Enhance Active Listening

**Present Moment Focus:** Practice focusing your attention on the speaker. This involves staying mentally present and fully engaged during conversations.

**Accepting Distractions:** Acknowledge when your mind wanders without judgment. Gently guide your focus back to the speaker.

**Reflecting on Values:** Consider how active listening aligns with your values, such as understanding or empathy, and let this guide your listening behavior.

**Observing Non-Verbal Cues:** Pay attention to non-verbal signals like body language and tone, aspects of active listening.

**Mindful Responses:** Formulate responses based on a genuine understanding of the speaker's message rather than reacting impulsively.

## Applying ACT to Manage Speaking Anxiety in Social Settings

**Recognizing Anxiety:** Notice feelings of nervousness or anxiety when speaking socially. Acknowledge these feelings without criticism.

**Mindful Breathing:** Use breathing techniques to stay calm and centered in social interactions, reducing anxiety.

**Value-Driven Conversations:** Focus on what you value in social interactions, like connection or sharing ideas, to guide your participation.

**Small-Step Engagement:** Start with low-pressure social settings and gradually work your way up to more challenging situations.

**Accepting Imperfection:** Embrace the idea that not every social interaction will be perfect. This acceptance can reduce the pressure and anxiety of social speaking.

# Additional Behavioral Techniques

In addition to Operant Conditioning and Acceptance and Commitment Therapy (ACT), other effective behavioral techniques exist that can complement these methods in improving communication skills.

## Cognitive Behavioral Therapy (CBT)

CBT plays a pivotal role in developing communication skills by emphasizing assertive, respectful, and honest interactions. It adapts communication methods based on the specific context and personal relationships involved. CBT effectively guides individuals to identify and modify their reactions to different communication styles, leading to a more assertive approach. Furthermore, it works on breaking down internal barriers that prevent assertive expression, such as self-limiting beliefs. This approach synergizes with the principles of ACT and Operant Conditioning, offering a comprehensive framework for enhancing communication abilities.

## Mindfulness-Based Stress Reduction (MBSR)

MBSR significantly improves communication skills by fostering a deeper sense of self-awareness and empathy. It helps you become attuned to your personal thoughts and feelings, as well as to the subtle indicators from those around you. This enhanced perception enables more thoughtful and measured responses instead of reactive or defensive ones. MBSR also nurtures empathetic understanding, essential for establishing trust and rapport with colleagues and clients. Moreover, it bolsters your ability to express emotions in a healthy manner and sharpens listening skills by reducing external and internal distractions, crucial for truly effective communication and fostering creative problem-solving and clearer understanding in professional settings.

## Solution-Focused Brief Therapy (SFBT)

SFBT can be effectively applied to enhance mindful speaking and communication skills. SFBT's goal-oriented nature aligns well with the development of specific, achievable communication goals. For instance, if someone wishes to become more assertive in their speech, SFBT can help them focus on present behaviors and formulate practical steps towards this goal. Techniques like miracle questions can encourage individuals to envision their ideal communication style, while scaling questions help gauge progress in their speaking abilities. Overall, SFBT's emphasis on immediate solutions and personal growth offers a practical framework for improving communication skills in a focused and time-efficient manner. This approach can be particularly effective in setting specific, attainable goals in speech improvement, complementing the goal-setting aspect of Operant Conditioning.

## Wrapping Up: Harnessing Behavioral Tools for Transformation

Of these techniques, I found Operant Conditioning and ACT therapy most helpful. Choose as many or as few of these techniques as you wish. Each approach, with its unique strengths, offers a pathway to not just better speaking habits but to a deeper understanding of yourself and your interactions with others. The power of mindful speaking extends beyond mere words; it influences relationships, self-perception, and your impact on the world. As you experiment with these methods, you're not only enhancing your ability to communicate but also enriching your life experiences.

This chapter isn't just about learning techniques; it's a gateway to personal transformation. The skills and insights you gain here have the potential to change not just how you speak, but how you live and connect with others. Embrace this journey with an open mind and heart and watch as the art of mindful speaking reshapes your world.

Which brings us to the impact speech has on our physical health. In the next chapter, we'll explore the neuroscience behind healthy habits beyond the obvious of exercise and eating the veggies that moms have been insisting we eat for the last 10,000 years.

# CHAPTER 11

## Optimize Your Physical Health

**"The greatest wealth is health."** —Virgil

This chapter explores simple ways to enhance your speaking skills by taking care of your health. It's about straightforward, everyday habits like getting enough sleep, exercising regularly, eating well, and staying hydrated. These habits not only keep your body healthy but also sharpen your mind, making you a better speaker. Let's learn how easy changes in your daily routine can have a big impact on your communication skills.

### Understanding the Link Between Physical Health and Communication

Physical health is not just a matter of the body. It's a complex interplay of physical, mental, and emotional wellness. Each aspect of your health – from the food you consume to the amount of sleep you get – has a profound impact on how you process thoughts, regulate emotions, and, ultimately, how you express yourself. When your body is well nourished, rested, and cared for, your mind functions at its best, allowing for more precise, more empathetic, and more effective communication.

## The Process of Improvement

The essence of this is to enjoy the process of enhancing your health. Perfection is neither the goal nor the expectation. Instead, the focus is on gradual, consistent improvement. It's about making small, manageable changes to your daily routines and observing how these changes positively affect your speaking. This process of improvement promotes a kind of mindfulness that pays attention not only to what you say but also how you care for the vessel that enables you to speak— your body.

## Physical Wellbeing and Its Influence on Communication

Your physical state acts as the foundation upon which your speaking skills are built. When you are physically well, you have more energy to devote to the art of communication. You can think more clearly, react more calmly, and engage more fully. Your thoughts become more coherent, and your words carry more weight. We will look at how specific aspects of physical health, such as sleep, nutrition, and exercise, directly contribute to this process.

## The Role of Emotional Regulation in Speaking

Emotional regulation is another critical component of effective communication, and your physical health heavily influences it. When your physical needs are met, you are better equipped to handle stress, manage your emotions, and stay present in your conversations. This emotional stability allows you to respond mindfully rather than to merely react. It allows you to listen actively and to articulate your thoughts with much greater empathy.

## Realizing Your Potential in the Speaking Arts

Ultimately, caring for your physical health is about unlocking your full potential in the speaking arts. It's about giving yourself the tools and strength to convey your messages with confidence and clarity. This chapter serves as a guide to recognizing and nurturing the deep-seated connection between your physical well-being and your ability to engage in mindful communication.

As we journey through this chapter, I invite you to view each health habit not as a chore but as a step towards realizing your full potential as a master of the speaking arts. Embrace this journey with enthusiasm, understanding that every effort you make in improving your physical health is a step towards becoming a more articulate, thoughtful, and effective speaker.

# The Foundation of Thought and Speech: Basic Health Habits

## Sleep

The importance of sleep cannot be overstated. It's during sleep that your brain processes the day's information, solidifies memories, and rejuvenates. More than this, it makes predictions, based on the day's experiences, on how best to prepare for the next day. As you sleep, your brain produces neurotransmitters, hormones, and vagus nerve impulses specifically tailored to act on these predictions, preparing you for the challenges you are most likely to face the next day. (Irwin, 2019). This process is similar to that which the brain uses to produce intuition. (Barrett, 2015)

Lack of sleep can lead to impaired memory, reduced cognitive function, and emotional instability. During deep sleep, the body produces and releases cytokines, proteins that help regulate the immune system and respond to infection, inflammation, and stress. When sleep is frequently cut short or interrupted, cortisol production is increased via the hypothalamus-pituitary-adrenal axis, and the production of cytokines becomes unbalanced. Underproduction of certain cytokines leaves you vulnerable to viral infections. Repeated overproduction of others contributes to the risk of contracting diseases of chronic inflammation, such as heart attacks, strokes, cancer, and Alzheimer's disease. (Irwin, 2019; Zielinski, 2022)

Understanding the neuroscience of the relationship between good health and sleep involves recognizing the intricate connections between the nervous system, immune function, and various physiological processes, all of which directly influence your ability to communicate effectively. Adequate sleep equips you with the mental clarity and emotional balance necessary for mindful speaking. Remember this as you journal or otherwise reflect on your progress toward mindful speaking. As I did this, I found that lack of sleep preceded my worst speaking. And I've spoken my best when sleep, exercise and nutrition were all on point. Good sleep helps you to process your thoughts clearly and express yourself coherently.

## Exercise

Exercise is a powerful tool for mental health. It releases endorphins, known as "feel-good" hormones, which reduce the perception of pain and trigger positive feelings in your body. Regular moderate exercise has been shown to reduce anxiety, depression, and negative mood by improving self-esteem and cognitive function. This directly translates to enhanced speaking abilities, as a clear and positive mind is more capable of effective communication. Exercise also improves concentration and attention, key components in delivering articulate and well-thought-out speeches.

## Nutrition and Hydration

As you know, your diet plays a significant role in physical

health. Brain health, too. Foods rich in omega-3 fatty acids, antioxidants, vitamins, and minerals provide the brain with the necessary nutrients to function at a high level. A well-nourished brain is more capable of processing information, problem-solving, and managing emotions. Hydration is equally important as even mild dehydration can impair brain function, affecting concentration, alertness, and short-term memory. A balanced diet and adequate hydration can significantly enhance your cognitive abilities, emotional control, and speaking skills.

## Accident Prevention

Accidents can have a lasting impact on one's physical and mental health. Injuries can lead to chronic pain, depression, or anxiety, which can hinder your ability to communicate effectively. Simple preventive measures like wearing seatbelts, following safety guidelines, and being mindful of your surroundings can go a long way in maintaining your overall health and safety, enhancing your ability to communicate. Think safety first, please.

## Sunshine

Exposure to natural light, especially in the morning, has profound effects on your body. It has several neurological and physiological effects that contribute to good health. Though the primary mechanism through which sunlight is thought to promote health is the synthesis of vitamin D, other mechanisms may be in play since supplementation with vitamin D falls short as a replacement for moderate exposure to sunlight. (Alfredsson, 2020). Sunlight helps regulate your sleep-wake cycle, improves mood, and increases alertness. By aligning your circadian rhythms through exposure to sunlight, you enhance your mental clarity and mood stability, both vital for effective communication. The morning light exposure can set a positive tone for the entire day, making you poised and articulate. As you stack these excellent habits together, you will find yourself spreading good vibes through your words and how you speak them.

## Temperance

Abstinence and moderation have their places. At this time, there are valid arguments that even small amounts of alcohol may cause cancer. Yet wine is used in the Mediterranean diet, seemingly with health advantages. (Barbería-Latasa, 2022). For our purposes, it is safe to say that excessive consumption of alcohol or any amount of smoking can have detrimental effects on your cognitive and emotional functions. These substances can impair judgment, reduce inhibitions, and cloud your thinking, negatively impacting your ability to communicate. Excessive alcohol adversely affects the prefrontal cortex of the brain. And even small amounts of alcohol stimulate the release of dopamine in the reward centers of the brain. This explains, in part, why people who have gotten into trouble by consuming too much alcohol go on to repeat the same drinking pattern habitually. If that sounds like you or someone you know, please get professional help and/or reach out to Alcoholics Anonymous expeditiously. You are in good company. I have personally seen students, businesspersons, doctors, paramedics, clergy, and people from all walks of life get the rehab they need to overcome addiction.

## Fresh Air

Fresh air has numerous benefits for your mental and physical health. It improves brain function and concentration and cleanses the lungs. Breathing in fresh air, as opposed to stale, recycled indoor air, enhances oxygen flow to the brain, improving clarity of thought and the ability to focus—both critical for effective speaking. If you are stuck in a smoggy area or affected by wildfire smoke, have an air purifier with a HEPA filter, at least for one room in your house. You will feel better physically and emotionally by breathing clean air. And it will show in your speech.

## Broad Sense of Spirituality

Spirituality is not an exact science. Least of all when it comes to finding an answer to the question, "Why all the suffering?" Still, to be human is to wonder about this. It is a deeply personal subject—and a touchy one at that.

In my residency program, a small group of hospital chaplains took turns rounding on patients with us. These chaplains were good! They came from very different backgrounds but were experts at connecting with people and helping patients and their families cope with trauma.

From these chaplains and by observing intense experiences in the emergency department, I learned being spiritually healthy is to have a sense of connection with someone or with a noble cause that will outlast both you and me. The noble cause can be an abstract one, like "love," "hope," or "kindness." The "someone" might include children, grandchildren, or the Creator.

These connections bring peace and emotional stability, central to mindful speaking. This broad sense of spirituality can also foster empathy, allowing you to better understand and connect with your audience when you speak. (Gad, 2022; Puchalski, 2018; Willemse, 2020)

## Adapting to Personal Circumstances

It's important to acknowledge that each person's life experience is unique. The key is to adapt these health habits to fit your own life. For instance, a young man I treated during my training had been paralyzed from the neck down in a car accident. He could not move his arms or legs. He could only move his upper neck and three fingers on his left hand. What do you think he does for exercise? He sings! (Kang, 2018; Tamplin, 2012)

Another example from my emergency room work is how nightshift staff adapt their circadian rhythms. We made a point of enjoying evening twilight as if it was dawn, work our shift, and treat the morning light as if it was sunset. To this day, if I must wake up when it's dark outside, I use a sunrise-simulating light alarm. At the time I set, it shines a subtle reddish light that gradually becomes brighter and more yellow. After 20 minutes, it adds the sounds of birds chirping. It's not ideal, but it's much better than those noisy alarms that startle you out of deep sleep at silly o'clock in the morning! (Giménez, 2010)

## Neuroplasticity: The Power to Adapt and Thrive

Adaptability is a testament to neuroplasticity—the brain's ability to adapt and change. Keeping a perspective, staying connected to others, and committing to a noble cause are essential in this journey.

## The Transformation of Sarah: From Fatigue to Eloquence

Sarah, an ambitious marketing executive, always struggled with public speaking. Despite her knowledge and passion, she often found herself unable to articulate her thoughts clearly during presentations. Her speech was sometimes muddled, and she regularly experienced anxiety and brain fog.

## The Turnaround Begins

Sarah's journey to better speaking began unintentionally. Concerned about her health, she decided to make simple changes to her lifestyle. She started by prioritizing sleep, aiming for at least seven hours a night. This small change had an immediate effect; she began waking up feeling more refreshed and alert.

## Incorporating Exercise and Nutrition

Next, Sarah incorporated regular exercise into her routine. She started with brisk morning walks, not only invigorating her physically but also clearing her mind, reducing her daily stress. She also revamped her diet, focusing on whole foods that boosted her energy levels and cognitive function.

## Hydration and Its Impact

Sarah also realized she wasn't drinking enough water throughout the day. As she increased her hydration, she noticed fewer headaches and greater concentration, especially important during her presentations.

## The Results: A More Confident Speaker

Over time, Sarah's health changes had a remarkable effect on her speaking. She noticed her thoughts were more coherent during meetings. Her presentations were clearer and more concise, and she engaged audiences with renewed confidence.

The anxiety and brain fog that once clouded her abilities had lifted.

## Wrapping Up: Health as a Foundation for Effective Communication

This chapter is about understanding that simple, everyday health habits can significantly enhance your speaking skills. Sarah's story is an example of how prioritizing sleep, exercise, nutrition, and hydration can transform not only your physical health but also your ability to communicate effectively.

As we continue to explore the connection between physical health and the art of mindful speaking, it's clear that a holistic approach is necessary. It's about balancing various aspects of health to optimize your speaking skills. Each aspect, from nutrition to spirituality, plays a unique part in shaping your ability to communicate effectively and mindfully.

Like Sarah, you have already embarked on this journey. By implementing healthy changes to your daily routine, you sharpen your mind and become a more eloquent and persuasive speaker.

# References:

Alfredsson, L., Armstrong, B. K., Butterfield, D. A., Chowdhury, R., de Gruijl, F. R., Feelisch, M., Garland, C. F., Hart, P. H., Hoel, D. G., Jacobsen, R., Lindqvist, P. G., Llewellyn, D. J., Tiemeier, H., Weller, R. B., & Young, A. R. (2020). Insufficient Sun Exposure Has Become a Real Public Health Problem. *International journal of environmental research and public health*, *17*(14), 5014. https://doi.org/10.3390/ijerph17145014

Barbería-Latasa, M., Gea, A., & Martínez-González, M. A. (2022). Alcohol, Drinking Pattern, and Chronic Disease. *Nutrients*, *14*(9), 1954. https://doi.org/10.3390/nu14091954

Barrett, L. F., & Simmons, W. K. (2015). Interoceptive predictions in the brain. *Nature reviews. Neuroscience*, *16*(7), 419–429. https://doi.org/10.1038/nrn3950

Gad, I., Tan, X. C., Williams, S., Itawi, S., Dahbour, L., Rotter, Z., Mitro, G., Rusch, C., Perkins, S., & Ali, I. (2022). The Religious and Spiritual Needs of Patients in the Hospital Setting Do Not Depend on Patient Level of Religious/Spiritual Observance and Should be Initiated by Healthcare Providers. *Journal of religion and health*, *61*(2), 1120–1138. https://doi.org/10.1007/s10943-020-01103-7

Giménez, M. C., Hessels, M., van de Werken, M., de Vries, B., Beersma, D. G., & Gordijn, M. C. (2010). Effects of artificial dawn on subjective ratings of sleep inertia and dim light melatonin onset. *Chronobiology international*, *27*(6), 1219–1241. https://doi.org/10.3109/07420528.2010.496912

Irwin M. R. (2019). Sleep and inflammation: partners in sickness and in health. *Nature reviews. Immunology*, *19*(11), 702–715. https://doi.org/10.1038/s41577-019-0190-z

Kang, J., Scholp, A., & Jiang, J. J. (2018). A Review of the Physiological Effects and Mechanisms of Singing. *Journal of voice: official journal of the Voice Foundation*, *32*(4), 390–395. https://doi.org/10.1016/j.jvoice.2017.07.008

Puchalski, C. M., King, S. D. W., & Ferrell, B. R. (2018). Spiritual Considerations. *Hematology/oncology clinics of North America*, *32*(3), 505–517. https://doi.org/10.1016/j.hoc.2018.01.011

Tamplin, J., Baker, F. A., Grocke, D., Brazzale, D. J., Pretto, J. J., Ruehland, W. R., Buttifant, M., Brown, D. J., & Berlowitz, D. J. (2013). Effect of singing on respiratory function, voice, and mood after quadriplegia: a randomized controlled trial. *Archives of physical medicine and rehabilitation*, *94*(3), 426–434. https://doi.org/10.1016/j.apmr.2012.10.006

Willemse, S., Smeets, W., van Leeuwen, E., Nielen-Rosier, T., Janssen, L., & Foudraine, N. (2020). Spiritual care in the intensive care unit: An integrative literature research. *Journal of critical care*, *57*, 55–78.
https://doi.org/10.1016/j.jcrc.2020.01.026

Zielinski, M. R., & Gibbons, A. J. (2022). Neuroinflammation, Sleep, and Circadian Rhythms. *Frontiers in cellular and infection microbiology*, *12*, 853096.
https://doi.org/10.3389/fcimb.2022.853096

# STEP FOUR

## GET CONNECTED

*Do your best to optimize the relationships at school, work, home, or wherever, that affect you. And if your best isn't good enough, request help from a friend or mentor. Seek a licensed professional counselor or physician if indicated. No one is perfect, and we all need help now and then. Look for ways to improve your connections. Doing so will lead to improvements in how well you listen and speak.*

# CHAPTER 12

## Optimize Your Connections

**"... all life is interrelated."** —Martin Luther King, Jr, Christmas Sermon at Ebenezer Baptist Church, Atlanta, Georgia, 1967.

In the hustle and bustle of an emergency room, where every second counts and every decision is crucial, lies a profound lesson about life and human connection. As a physician navigating the complexities of ER dynamics, I came to realize that amidst the chaos, sometimes the most potent medicine isn't found in the drugs we administer but in the connections we forge with patients, their families, and colleagues.

This chapter unfolds the art of optimizing these human connections, drawing insights from the heart of emergency medicine.

# The Essence of Human Connection

Human connection is of paramount importance for various aspects of individual well-being and societal development. Human connections provide a support system, celebrating achievements during positive moments and offering emotional support during times of crisis. Nowhere is this more prevalent than in a healthcare setting.

## Embracing Empathy in Tragedy

Picture the ER in the aftermath of a tragic accident. A family huddles, grieving the loss of a child. In these moments, our role transcends medical intervention. It's about holding space, sharing their sorrow, and offering a shoulder to cry on. This vignette isn't just about the pain; it's a stark reminder that all of us are mortal and there is a time to grieve.

## Celebrating Life Together

In contrast, envision the overwhelming joy when we successfully revive a patient in cardiac arrest. The family's tears of fear transform into tears of joy. Here, our connection lies in shared relief and happiness, reinforcing the power of teamwork and collective hope.

## Witnessing Recovery and Renewal

Consider the stroke patient who, against all odds, regains speech and mobility. Their triumph isn't just a personal victory;

it's a collective celebration of human resilience, reminding us of our shared potential for recovery and growth.

### The Ripple Effect of a Single Act

Reflect on reversing an opioid overdose with naloxone. Sometimes, it's not just the medical intervention but the subsequent interaction that leaves a lasting impact. A few encouraging words can ignite a spark of hope, inspiring a journey towards healing and self-improvement.

## The Journey from Helplessness to Empowerment

Each of us, regardless of our current stature – a renowned botanist, respected leader,  hardworking mechanic – began life as a helpless infant. This universal truth underscores our inherent interconnectedness and mutual dependence. In the ER, this reality is starkly evident as we work shoulder to shoulder with diverse individuals, each carrying their own story, yet bound by common needs for survival, respect, and affection.

## Communication: The Heart of Connection

The art of speaking and listening is crucial in the ER. We've touched upon this in earlier chapters but let's dig deeper. Consider practicing a speaking fast, where, for a day or two, you limit your words to the barest essentials. This exercise can enhance your listening skills, help you develop the new habit of pausing before you speak, and make your words more impactful.

# Practical Tips for Optimizing Connections

No matter the profession, networking and building relationships are essential for career advancement, mentorship, teamwork, collaboration, and emotional well-being.

### Fostering Open Communication in the Workplace

In high-pressure environments like the ER, the collective wisdom of the team is a valuable asset. To foster open communication:

**Create a Safe Space for Dialogue:** Establish a workplace environment where team members can freely express their opinions and concerns without fear of criticism or backlash. This can be fostered through consistent team meetings and systems for anonymous feedback.

**Lead by Example:** Leaders should actively demonstrate open communication, showing that every team member's perspective is valued. This involves actively seeking input from all levels of staff and acknowledging their contributions.

**Encourage Diverse Perspectives:** Recognize that diverse viewpoints can lead to better problem-solving. Encourage team members from different backgrounds and with different levels of experience to share their insights.

**Implement Regular Debriefings:** After critical incidents, hold debriefings where everyone can discuss what happened, what went well, and what could be improved. This not only enhances learning but reinforces the value of each team member's input.

## The Power of Closed-Loop Communication

In environments where miscommunication can have serious consequences, closed-loop communication is essential:

**Clarify and Confirm:** Encourage team members to repeat back instructions or information received to confirm understanding. This is the essence of closed-loop communication. Its practice should be normalized and encouraged at all levels.

**Train for Clarity:** Offer training sessions focused on effective communication techniques, including how to give clear instructions and how to ask for clarification without hesitation.

**Use Checklists and Protocols:** Implement checklists and standardized communication protocols, especially for complex or routine procedures, to ensure all steps are clearly communicated and followed.

## Home Life Balance: Embracing Simplicity and Mindfulness

After a demanding shift in the ER, the transition back to home life can be tough, both physically and emotionally. Consider this scenario as an exemplary way to achieve balance:

**Decompressing Post-Shift:** Imagine the scenario of returning home after an intense ER shift. The journey itself, often accompanied by traffic, can be taxing. It's important to use this time to gradually transition from the high-stress environment of the ER to the tranquility of home. This could involve listening to calming music or a podcast, practicing deep breathing, or simply enjoying the silence.

Oh, and here's some urban traffic culture to remember: while enjoying the ride home, singing along to your favorite end-of-shift playlist, you might encounter a less-than-courteous driver who nearly collides with you. Resist the urge to express your frustration with an offensive gesture. We don't need any more road rage incidents. Should you find your dominant hand involuntarily rising and clenching into a fist with a particular finger edging forward, quickly morph this gesture into something more graceful; perhaps a peace sign or use it to cross yourself in the Christian way. It's much safer than flipping an angry stranger the middle finger. You are trying to reach home, remember? We do not want to have to return to the ER as a patient.

**Mindful Engagement at Home:** Once home, instead of immediately immersing yourself in household chores or other responsibilities, take a moment for yourself. This might mean sitting down on the floor and engaging playfully with your toddler. Such actions aren't just about unwinding; they're an exercise in mindfulness. Being present in these moments, with playful talk and laughter, can be incredibly grounding and rejuvenating.

**The Value of Simple Acts:** The simple act of sitting with your child, devoid of the complexities of your professional role, serves as a powerful reminder of life's basic joys. It's in these uncomplicated interactions that you often find the most joy.

**Nurturing Family Bonds:** Engaging in simple yet meaningful activities not only helps in decompressing from the stresses of work but also strengthens the bond with your family. It's a reminder that sometimes, the most impactful connections are the ones we nurture through our presence and simple, heartfelt interactions.

## Connecting with Your Partner

Maintaining a strong, healthy relationship with your partner requires conscious effort and communication:

**Regular Check-ins:** Set aside time for regular check-ins with your partner to talk about each other's day, feelings, and any concerns. This should be a time free from distractions and interruptions.

**Active Listening:** Practice active listening, where you fully concentrate, understand, and respond thoughtfully to what your partner is saying. This builds a deeper connection and understanding between you.

**Express Appreciation and Affection:** Frequently showing gratitude and affection to your partner is essential for a healthy relationship. Simple, yet meaningful expressions of appreciation can profoundly strengthen your bond.

**Seek Balance Between Giving and Receiving:** Ensure a balance in your relationship where both partners feel heard, supported, and valued.

By implementing these practical tips, we can optimize our connections across all aspects of our lives, fostering environments of mutual respect, understanding, and support.

# Wrapping Up: Embracing the Journey of Improvement

Reflect on the process of optimizing your connections, both in our professional lives and at home. It's important to approach each step in the right direction with a sense of positivity and enthusiasm. The journey towards better communication and stronger relationships is ongoing, and every small step forward is a victory in itself.

Remember, improvement is not just a destination but a continuous path that you travel. Each day brings new opportunities to enhance the way you connect with others. Whether it's fostering open communication in the workplace, practicing closed-loop communication to avoid misunderstandings, or finding balance in your home life, each effort contributes to a larger tapestry of personal and professional growth.

It's essential to celebrate your progress, no matter how small it may seem. Every time you successfully implement a new communication strategy, every moment you spend mindfully with your family, and every heartfelt conversation with your partner, are milestones worth recognizing. These achievements not only boost your morale but also reinforce the importance of the journey you're on – to improve your ability to converse.

Moreover, allow yourself the grace to learn from experiences that don't go as planned. Each challenge is an opportunity to grow and refine your approach to building and sustaining connections. The key is to remain open, adaptable, and forgiving, both to yourself and others, as you navigate this path.

Begin to embrace the joy and fulfillment that comes from improving and deepening your connections. Let this journey be one of discovery, where you not only learn more about effective communication and relationship building but also uncover new facets of yourself and those around you. Continue to move forward with a positive mindset, cherishing each step in this enriching process of personal and professional growth.

Let's continue on this noble path as we move onto the importance of mentors and mentorship in the next chapter.

# CHAPTER 13

## Enlist the Help of a Mentor

**"... have someone whom you may look up to, someone whom you may regard as a witness of your thoughts."**
—Seneca

In the journey of personal growth and mastering the art of communication, one of the most transformative steps you can take is to seek guidance from those who have walked the path before you. Mentors act as beacons, illuminating the way forward with their wisdom and experience. They remind us that we do not have to face our challenges alone and that, in the rich tapestry of human interaction, learning from others is not just helpful—it's essential.

I have been blessed with mentors at several stages of my life. One such mentor was found on short notice during medical school. Instructors were allowed to be tougher back then—to the point of being verbally abusive by today's standards. I will change the names so as not to hurt people who have improved since then. I'll call the instructor, Dr. Betyde.

## Facing Challenges: Learning and Growing with Dr. Betyde

In my medical school days, the atmosphere was often tense. At times, stress ran high, and the stakes felt monumental. One instructor stood out for his particularly daunting reputation among the many professors and physicians. Dr. Betyde. He was mean.

To Dr. Betyde, the medicine world was a relentless battlefield. Mistakes were as unforgivable as they were inevitable. By today's standards, his approach was nothing short of verbally abusive. He was undoubtedly clinically excellent, but his harsh demeanor and haste to blame made rotations under his watch a dreaded experience. Word of his reputation spread through our class like a chilling wind. As my rotation under him approached, the anxiety within me grew.

However, amidst the whispers and worried glances of my classmates, there was Brian. He was a "B" student with an "A+" in emotional intelligence. As a classmate, Brian kept a calm demeanor in the face of frankly abusive teachers. Brian had recently completed a rotation with Dr. Betyde. He had emerged seemingly unscathed, a feat that seemed nearly impossible to the rest of us. As it turned out, his secret was a blend of wit, humility, and an unexpected strategy. When I sought out Brian for advice, he shared his approach with a laugh, "Dr. Betyde is easy! Apologize immediately for anything that goes wrong, even if it's clearly not your fault." This advice sounded risky, almost counterintuitive, but Brian's confidence and the success of his rotation convinced me to try. I informed the other classmates on the rotation what I was up to and where I got the idea.

A week later, as I stood in the operating room, retractor in hand, the moment of truth arrived. Far from my direct involvement, a small error occurred, yet I remembered Brian's advice and apologized. Dr. Betyde's reaction was a moment of silent intensity, a glance that felt like it could pierce through steel. A few minutes later, a nurse on the other side of the operating room dropped a sterile instrument to the floor. I immediately apologized for it. At that point, Dr. Betyde put both hands down on the sterile draped belly of the patient, looked at me and my classmates, and said in a somewhat friendly tone, "OK. I know what's going on." Something had shifted. Dr. Betyde began to soften, his voice losing the sharp edge of constant criticism. It was as if acknowledging the imperfection in all of us, including himself, allowed him to breathe, to step back from the precipice of relentless judgment.

This change wasn't just noticeable to me. Over time, Dr. Betyde's demeanor changed for the better. The relentless critic began to show moments of humor, even camaraderie. He brought his daughter to rounds, revealing glimpses of life and personality beyond the stern facade. It was as if a door had been unlocked, revealing a more complex and humane individual beneath the armor of criticism.

Brian's insights and his emotional intelligence had not only helped me navigate a challenging rotation but had also, in some small way, contributed to a shift in Dr. Betyde's interaction with all students. The mentorship I received from Brian extended beyond tactics and strategies; it was a lesson in empathy, resilience, creativity, and the power of understanding human behavior.

This experience was a vivid illustration of the necessity of mentorship and the profound impact it can have. As humans, our growth and learning are deep social processes. We absorb not just the knowledge but the attitudes, approaches, and even the coping mechanisms of those around us. Therefore, seeking mentors is not just about improving a particular skill or navigating a specific challenge. It's about consciously choosing who influences your development and aligning yourself with individuals who embody the qualities and values you admire. It's about finding someone who understands your journey. In this way, mentorship becomes a pivotal part of your own narrative, a shared journey of growth, discovery, and becoming a better version of yourself.

# Insights and Strategies for Growth

The experience with Dr. Betyde and the guidance from Brian brought to light several profound realizations about communication, mentorship, and personal growth. These insights serve as lessons and practical tips for anyone looking to navigate similar challenges.

## Understanding Human Dynamics

Behind every harsh exterior lies a complex set of emotions and experiences. I learned that even the most intimidating figures are human at heart by approaching Dr. Betyde with empathy and strategic communication.

When dealing with difficult people, try to understand what drives their behavior. Instead of reacting defensively, use empathy and strategic communication to disarm tension and foster a more positive interaction.

## The Power of Apology

Apologizing, even when not at fault, is like a spice best used sparingly. It can defuse tension and shift dynamics. It's not about accepting blame but showing a willingness to take responsibility and move forward.

Consider using apologies to shift the focus from blame to resolution in tense situations. This doesn't mean undermining your self-worth but strategically steering the conversation towards a more constructive outcome.

## Seeking and Embracing Mentorship

Actively seek mentors who excel in their field and embody the emotional and communicative skills you aspire to develop. Be bold, ask for guidance, and be open to learning from their experiences.

## The Ripple Effect of Change

Change in one's behavior can influence others in unexpected ways. My approach influenced Dr. Betyde's behavior, creating a more favorable environment for everyone.

Recognize the impact of your actions and words on others. Small changes in your behavior can create positive ripples in your environment. It is said that each person on the planet is no more than 6 or 7 connections away from anyone else. What you do and say, and how you go about it, affects everyone. We are indeed related to each other.

## Continuous Personal Development

The journey of personal and professional development is an ongoing one. Every experience is an opportunity to learn and grow.

Reflect on each experience and seek the lesson within. Continuously seek growth opportunities, and don't shy away from challenging situations—they are often where the most valuable lessons are learned.

## Fostering a Supportive Community

Being part of a community where people uplift each other is crucial for growth. Brian's support was a testament to the power of a supportive peer network.

Surround yourself with individuals who are not only skilled and knowledgeable but also supportive and positive. Be that person for others as well; a supportive community is built on mutual respect and encouragement.

## Embracing Vulnerability

Showing vulnerability, like apologizing when not at fault, can be a strength. It demonstrates openness and a readiness to engage and improve, which can transform relationships and environments.

Don't be afraid to show your human side, including your uncertainties and mistakes. This doesn't mean you should take the blame unnecessarily, but being open about your learning process can encourage others to be more understanding and supportive, fostering a more collaborative and positive environment.

195

# Wrapping Up: Moving Forward – Harnessing Insights for Future Success

The lessons learned from the rotation with Dr. Betyde, underpinned by Brian's mentorship, extend far beyond medical training. They are about understanding human behavior, the power of communication, and the importance of empathy and strategic thinking. These insights are universally applicable, offering valuable strategies for anyone navigating complex personal and professional landscapes. Embrace these lessons and practical tips to enhance your journey towards mindful communication and continuous personal growth.

# CHAPTER 14

## Remember the Pearl

**"Pleasant words are a honeycomb, sweet to the soul, and health to the bones."** —Solomon. (Proverbs 16:24, World English Bible)

To reinforce the art of mindful speaking, I sought symbols and reminders that I could wear or post in various places. One such symbol is the pearl—a lustrous gem that emerges from a wounded, imperfect heart of irritation. I think it is a well-suited reminder in that regard. Whether you choose the pearl or symbology of your own, I nevertheless invite you to include a pearl or artwork featuring a pearl to keep you on track.

## The Pearl as a Metaphor

Imagine the oyster, nestled in the dark sea, suddenly invaded by an irritant. Rather than succumbing to this discomfort, it responds by creating something beautiful. The pearl's serene beauty and understated elegance testify to the oyster's resilience. Similarly, our lives are full of potential irritants: time pressure, harsh words, misunderstandings, and the daily frictions of human interaction. Like the oyster, we can envelope these challenges with layers of patience, understanding, and kindness, transforming them into pearls of wisdom and experience.

## Integrating the Pearl into Daily Life

How can we keep this metaphor alive in our everyday interactions? One way is by physically surrounding ourselves with reminders. Perhaps it's a pearl ring that glints in the sunlight, catching your eye and reminding you of the beauty of patience. If it's a masculine look you need, simply use the search term "masculine pearl bracelet" as a starter. I do not receive any royalty for the endorsement, but I found such a bracelet from an online store called Alton of Sweden.

Another option could be to hang a print of Rembrandt's "Girl with a Pearl Earring" in your office, her gaze constantly reminding you to respond to life's irritations with poise and creativity. Even a photo of a pearl cut from the pages of a magazine can be displayed at your work site as a free reminder. On your desk, a single pearl can be placed as a tactile reminder of the smooth, rounded beauty you strive to embody in your conversations and reactions.

## The Beauty of Process

Remembering the pearl also means appreciating the process. Just as a pearl is formed over time, through multiple layers of response to irritation, so is our ability to speak mindfully and listen with intent. It's a practice, a layering of skills and virtues built one upon the other. Wear your pearl jewelry or display your art not just as an ornament but as a badge of honor, representing your commitment to growth and the understanding that beauty and wisdom come from facing life's irritations head-on.

## A Symbol for All

Finally, remember that the pearl is a universal symbol, transcending cultures and ages. It reminds us that the journey to refine our speech and our responses is a shared human endeavor. Whether you're a teenager feeling the sting of social pressures or an elder reflecting on a life full of complex conversations, the pearl's lesson is for you. It's a reminder that within each of us lies the potential to create something valuable and beautiful from the grit of everyday life.

# Wrapping Up: Transforming Challenges into Treasures

In life, just like in conversation, reacting quickly and without much thought is straightforward. But you are changing that. You have come to know yourself more fully. You have gone a day or two without speaking and have learned from that. You have shaped your habits to reflect who you are. You can now transform every challenge into something valuable instead of just reacting. Not that you are perfect. But, like a diamond with a unique inclusion or a pearl with its grain of sand, you add value to this old planet of ours.

Think of the pearl as a piece of jewelry and as a symbolic mentor. It's a reminder that you're not merely reacting to what life throws at you. Instead, you're taking each moment, each irritation, and crafting it into something beautiful. When you wear a pearl or keep an image of one close, and some irritation comes your way, take a deep breath and glance at the pearl. Let it nudge your thoughts and words in a creative and productive direction. It's a symbol of your ability to change and adapt, turning challenging situations into opportunities for growth.

The oyster doesn't know it's creating a pearl. It's just responding to its environment in the only way it knows how. There's wisdom in that—the wisdom of persistence and quiet determination. When you're practicing mindful speaking, think of the oyster. Embrace its lesson: keep working and keep covering life's irritants with layers of patience, understanding, and care. Over time, you'll transform these irritants into pearls of wisdom.

Every time you speak, you have a choice. More precisely, through self-discovery, inner healing, and rewiring your brain with good habits, you have created the ability to choose. You can react quickly. Or you can pause, think, and respond in a way that adds value to the conversation. Imagine each word you speak as part of a pearl you're creating. With this image in your heart and mind, start your conversations confidently. You're not just talking. Your conscious and subconscious mind, habits, and body are working in concert to speak authentically and effectively. You are crafting something beautiful—the creative, healing vibrations of spoken words.

Printed in Great Britain
by Amazon